FAREHAM
BETWEEN
THE WARS

by

Alice James

Published by Paul Cave Publications Ltd.,
74 Bedford Place, Southampton, Hants.

Printed by Brown and Son (Ringwood) Ltd.

1

£4.50

TO JIMMY

ISBN 0-86146-077-4

First published in November, 1989

Cover design by Robin Pelling

CONTENTS

The Armistice procession through the streets of Fareham – marking the jubilation and relief at the end of the 1914-18 World War.

Introduction

To the visitor or 'incomer', in the 21 years (1918-1939) between the two terrible wars, Fareham seemed a typical Hampshire market town with its wide West Street, its Georgian High Street and its passages or drokes often leading to courts and yards containing anything from four to forty cottages. Busy on market day, it seemed to relax and even go to sleep for the rest of the week; surrounded mainly by rich farm lands and by the sea in the south.

True, one guide book dated 1929, stated that Fareham was 'a singularly unattractive little town' and that it had 'two churches, neither of which need detain the visitor'; but this guide book was the exception. Most extolled Fareham's past prosperity, pleasant streets and shops and its picturesque and still busy quays. One guide book, looking ahead from 1928, forecast accurately Fareham's future importance as 'a junction between inland towns and villages and the coast'.

This development was yet to come. In 1919 and the early 1920s Fareham, like all other small communities, was endeavouring to come to terms with the grievous loss of lives and the hardships of the Great War. There were still shortages, people were tired and run down, the children had suffered and in parts of the town there was great poverty and hardship only made bearable by the genuine kindness of neighbours and the warmth of a small community.

Life was never going to be the same again. Many facets of life of pre-1914 were gone, never to return. Old traditional industries were ending partly because of the shortage of labour. Tanning and brick making were two casualties and the town stagnated until new industries developed.

One Fareham resident, the late Mr. J. P. Garrad, saw 1918 as the end of class distinction, particularly as far as shopping was concerned. He commented "Pre-war, wives of retired officers, bank managers or other carriage folk would never have got out of their carriages when shopping and one of the first things I noticed on returning after the war was that these people were doing their own shopping and carrying their own parcels home. Illustrative of this spirit, there was a well known case when one of these people wrote to the paper and asked that why when things were so scarce, meat should not be reserved for those who were always used to having it, and should not be sold to poor people who were used to making a meal of bloaters. I should hate to guess how many bloaters were put through her letter box afterwards!"

The end of class distinction did not seem to apply elsewhere. In the big houses, life below stairs or behind the baize door could be extremely hard. For example at 'Uplands' in the late 1920s, there was an 'indoor' staff of five and the regular day lasted from 5.30 a.m. until 10 p.m. and there was no overtime payment if there were dinner parties. A kitchen maid never once saw her mistress in three years and worked for £26 per year. The cook got £36. In spite of this, the comment was "the food was good". The gardeners, thinning grapes, had to wait until the cool of the evening before they could work in the greenhouses, but there was no extra pay. At Cams Hall, even prior to the Second World War, similar harsh conditions prevailed. At Lysses House in the High Street, conditions were much better.

The owners of these houses were pillars of local society, philanthropists, honest and caring school managers and workhouse trustees. Many were also magistrates. They demanded due deference from 'lesser folk' but were on nodding acquaintance with the 'better sort' although they did not invite them to take part in social gatherings.

Yet coming through all the comments is the thread that life in Fareham was happy — "Fareham was a friendly place . . . we all knew each other . . . we helped each other . . . we knew where to go for help . . . we knew he would speak for us". These phrases occur again and again.

Is it just distance lending enchantment? I think not, because too many of the harsh realities are also clearly remembered.

A. J.

The Avenue.

The Town

In 1918, Fareham, as a town, was fairly compact with West Street, High Street, and Quay Street marking the old town. Prior to the Great War, additional building had taken place. Trinity Street and Park Lane were developing, the latter having changed its name from Puxol Lane, and the famous Price's School was well established in the place where it was to remain for eighty years. School Road, later to become Gordon Road; Osborn Road and Portland Street had been completed. Southampton Road had been laid out in lots for a group of people who had formed themselves into the 'County of Hants Freehold Land Society'. Then they had drawn lots for the ownership of the different plots of land. Town planning with a difference!

There were also scattered cottages and houses along Old Turnpike, Wickham Road, Kiln Road and North Hill, often connected with the pottery and clay pipe industries. Others were to be found grouped around the quays, where there were also several large houses.

This was Fareham immediately after the Great War. Afterwards and with gathering momentum in the 1930s, came more extensive building along Gosport Road, Deans Park Road, Serpentine Road and their surroundings, together with the Redlands Estate.

Leading into Fareham from the west, the tree lined Avenue, with its large houses well set back from the road and in large gardens, made a beautiful entrance and prosperous introduction to the town.

From older residents often not at all well off when young, and having large families, we do also hear of the quiet kindnesses of families in the big houses of this area. Mr. and Mrs. W. O. Smith, who lived at Charlfred in the Avenue, did a lot of good work. They brought fruit from their orchard and would get some of the older children to help to weed the garden, sending them home with money, vegetables and flowers after first giving them a good home-made tea.

Nearer the town, large houses included the imposing Blackbrook House, home of Sir William and Lady Parker (who were always there in time of need with great barrels of logs to help to keep families warm in winter) and Blackbrook Grove, which in 1927 was to become the home of the newly created Bishop of Portsmouth and renamed Bishopswood. Across the road was 'Redlands', home of Colonel Quarry. It had beautiful gardens with peacocks on the lawns. Colonel Quarry loved children; started the Scouts and gave them the Scout Hut and helped in many other ways. When the peacocks got out into the road or even into the trees of Bishopswood, he would pay the children 'coppers' (pence) to chase them back into the garden.

One of Fareham's old toll houses stood at the corner of West Street and Gudge Heath Lane. It was still there into the 1960s.

Redlands House had a large staff including a coachman, the lawns and gardens ran down to Avenue Road and at the bottom of the garden were fresh water springs and lily ponds. Living opposite to them in Oakcroft (now Croft House) the Misses Taylor's were district visitors for this area. If a baby was expected, baby clothes were often provided and a pram if needed. They also sent along apples from their orchard.

Paxton Road is an excellent example of some of the older terraced houses with its shop and Post Office and which, together with other small terraces, formed a complete local community near the railway station. It had its own public house, the original West End Inn, which was rebuilt after the Great War only to be pulled down in 1968 when the road was widened.

Nearby were the Cremer Cottages, four alms houses built by Sir William Cremer. He was born in Fareham, educated by his mother and was destined to become a Member of Parliament. Founder of the Peace Palace at the Hague, he was also a Nobel Peace Prize winner.

Blackbrook House.

8

This picture of Titchfield Road toll-gate was, of course, taken before the First World War but the toll-gate remained until the 1960s.
Below: Paxton Road.

The Railway Station.

The railway station, built by Thomas Brassey, had an imposing and sweeping entrance and boasted its own Railway Hotel. Until 1929, it marked the terminus of the Gosport-Fareham Tramway and by 1921 it had its own taxi rank.

It might be thought by readers, that the accompanying picture of the railway entrance is distinctly old fashioned, but in fact this scene was to remain the same until well after the Second World War.

Below: Tramway Terminus.

10

The taxi stand at Fareham Station on July 10, 1921. Below: another Fareham taxi-cab (this photograph was taken on June 12, 1921).

The Fareham 'Hunt'. Ready for the off!

The Railway Hotel was regularly the scene of a cheerful event on Boxing Day, when 'the lads of the village' otherwise known as the 'Fareham Hunt' gathered, together with hounds of indiscriminate breeds in front of the hotel. Aided and abetted by the landlord in more ways than one, and led by Mr. W. Sandys, who was always on horseback, they set off merrily towards the fields around Titchfield. Bets were laid on the 'bag' which was due to be raffled. However, and not surprisingly, they rarely returned with anything. In 1935, the 'bag' was a hedgehog!

Below: On the trail.

West End – tree lined West Street.

From here, apart from a few shops at West End, West Street remained residential and tree lined. On the right hand side of West Street a handsome terrace of houses with railed gardens were occupied by so many naval officers or retired officers and their families that it became known as 'Admirals' Row'. During the 1930s, the ground floors of some of these houses became shops, but the upper floors still retained their old character.

Below: another view of the western end of West Street.

13

The Town's War Memorial being dedicated in 1921.

From here, the real Fareham market town started and we have the basis of what was later to become Fareham's Golden Mile. Holy Trinity Church with its tall spire, stood out clearly and next to it was the large Church House. The War Memorial was erected in front of the church, dedicated in 1921 and unveiled by Earl Haig.

The Armistice jubilations marked the general relief of the end of four long, hard years. 'Guns Week' in Fareham commenced on Monday, November 11th and it was considered a happy co-incidence that the opening day should have proved to have been the most momentous in the history of nations. As the glorious news got about, joy was depicted on every countenance and quickly West Street and other thoroughfares became be-flagged. The outside of the Fire Station was made bright with flags and flowers.

In the evening an Armistice demonstration was held. After the German flag had been burned a procession was formed headed by the Fire Brigade, followed by an illuminated lorry belonging to Mr. Dyke. A great crowd had assembled despite the rain. The principal street lamps had been cleaned owing to the 'Lights up' order, and the flaming arc lamps, seen for the first time for many months, cut the gloom into many patterns. Music was blown from toy trumpets, there was much waving of flags and altogether it was a night to remember. The day's procession had included three pairs of horsed-trollies and other vehicles, decorated with flags and packed with children. Army men, nurses, Girl Guides and Boy Scouts also joined the procession. The latter provided the drum and fife band.

The First World War victory celebrations.

"On the next evening the rejoicing continued. Fireworks were discharged, miniature guns were fired and soldiers and civilians joined in the innocent scenes of 'Mafeking', which caused great fun. The military patients in the local hospitals, for example Hawkestone House, have entered with vim into the spirit of exultation." (Thus recorded the *Hampshire Telegraph.*) No doubt the jollifications were helped by the numerous pubs in the vicinity — the Red Lion, Kings Head, Bugle, Crown, and White Horse to name but a few!

We digress . . . this was a period when people were still making their own amusements. Many of these were held in connection with different churches and Sunday Schools. Amateur theatricals, concerts, socials and dramatic readings all played their part. Church House was the centre for many performances which were to be held right into the years after the Second World War. There were also private invitation dances and these were usually arranged by the girls from what were the four larger drapers' shops — Warns, Shillings, Phillips and Letherens. The boys gave a return dance. Strict rules regarding dress and behaviour were observed and the dances usually continued until 2 a.m. These particular dances were held at the Forester's Hall.

There were also regular fairs, fetes, Sunday School outings and, of course, Fareham Regatta. Regular sports days were held and great was the excitement when the circus came to town.

Such entertainments continued well into the 1930s; dances were held at the Connaught Drill Hall, Foresters Hall, Portland Hall and the Red Lion. Fareham had two enterprising amateur dance bands.

15

Top. Entertainment at Church House, amongst those present were: Mrs. Winnett, Mrs. Lunn, Mrs Mann, Mrs. Isaacs, Mrs. Nash, Mrs. Parker, Mrs. Albrow, Mrs. Patterson, Miss Hackney, Miss Frost and Miss Orange-Bromhead.
The same ladies appear in the picture below.

The Fareham Fanciers and Horticultural Show, 1928, at the Connaught Drill Hall.
Below: The Horticultural Show of 1937.

Among the prosperous and often family shops in this area were still the private houses of Fareham residents. A 1930 list shows the names of Trigg, Nicholson, Hayter and Bishop to name but a few. Mr. Coghlan lived at 'Milestone' just opposite Mr. Job, the jeweller. By Mr. Coghlan's house stood the old milestone from turnpike days. It still survives set into the wall of a restaurant.

On the opposite side of the road and quite near to Osborn Road was Malthouse Lane. It was a droke or passage, paved entirely with malthouse tiles and with a group of houses in one of which Mr. Whiting, the sweep lived. Remnants of the lane can still be seen when entering the present Osborn Road car park. Beer's music shop stood on the corner; here instruments, gramophones and records, and sheet music were readily available.

The Post Office 'wandered' about considerably. It had started at Nicholson's the printers (later Vimpany's), relatively near High Street. It had a post box inside the shop and letters were posted through a hole in the counter. It then moved to a position across the road from the top of Portland Street. It finally came to rest (we thought) opposite the top of Hartlands Road where it remained during the period covered by this book.

Opposite the Post Office, on the corner of Hartlands Road, were the premises of Sidney Smith, the photographer, from whose glass negatives we have obtained many of our photographs.

Murray's, the gentleman's outfitter, sold everything a man could want and Mr. Murray, already a J.P. and a well respected businessman, served in the shop. He was destined to do so until he was well over eighty years old.

Below: The General Post Office.

This photograph, taken in 1960, shows how West Street was in the 1930s. The bay windows of the White Horse can be seen clearly as can the old Post Office. Below: an earlier view of the General Post Office.

Modern times were coming. Before the Great War, Mr. Garrad had seen 'moving pictures' at a show given in the yard of the Bugle Inn. When a chapel near the old Post Office was pulled down, Fareham's Electrical Theatre was built. It showed 'The Count of Monte Christo' in serial form. A cliff-hanger indeed! Later, in 1923, the cinema was to re-open as the Alexandra Theatre. When refurbished in 1928, it was opened by the Vicar of Holy Trinity, Rev. Andrew Hargrave. It finally closed in 1933, but by then the Savoy Cinema had been built. A terrace together with the cinema, known as the Savoy Buildings, was built on the site of Westbury House lands.

The Savoy Cinema, built in 1933, also had an extremely good restaurant. It was followed by the building of the Embassy Cinema in 1938, on the site of the old Alexandra. This was the height of the cinema period before the Second World War and both cinemas were packed nightly, often with long queues waiting patiently ("Two seats available in the 1/9s!").

On the opposite side of Westbury Passage stood a large house and solicitor's office. It was later to become a dental surgery, the dentist being named Mr. Butcher. Westbury Passage led to Westbury Farm and its fields, and the farm buildings remain to the present day. Westbury House, very large and having large gates on either side of the property, had huge gardens. It was the home of Mrs. Matthews, widow of Lieut. Col. Matthews.

Opposite stood Westbury Manor, equally large but considerably older. It was another gracious home with large gateways leading to West Street and big gardens extending southwards flanked by Hartlands Road. It was owned in 1920 by Dame Madeleine Eva Waistell, wife of Admiral A.K. Waistell, whose distinguished naval career included being A.D.C. to the King, Commander-in-Chief of the China Station in 1929 and Commander-in-Chief Portsmouth in 1931. The house was sold to Fareham Urban District Council in 1932.

Admiral Waistell had one of the few cars around in the mid-20s and his garage exit, which was into Hartlands Road, was high above road level and required a wooden ramp. The Admiral reversed his car out with the help of his wife's guidance but frequently reversed too rapidly and hit the lamp post on the opposite side of the road. While he lived in the house that lamp post was always leaning!

Beyond Westbury Manor were a few more shops and the magnificent Wesleyan Church, which stood imposingly at the top of a flight of steps. Then, bordering on Portland Street stood three cottages, one of which had been the home of Thackeray's great aunt. These cottages were pulled down prior to the Second World War to make way for a bus station, as previously the buses had been parked in the centre of West Street. Slates from the cottages were actually used on the bus station buildings.

The coming of the cinema. Above: This was the original Electrical Theatre to be renamed the Alexandra Theatre in 1923. Below: The Savoy.

21

A panoramic view of West Street beyond Portland Street gives us a good general idea of the length and width of this fine street. It allows us to realise how animals which had been kept in fields in the Park Lane and Red Barn Lane areas overnight, could be driven down and even sold in the street. They added considerably to traffic on Market Day.

It is interesting to note that Portland Street itself was only destined to last for just over a hundred years. At this time it was a busy street with the tramway from Gosport.

The Portland Chambers (an early 19th century building) has had many names including the Town Hall, Corn Hall, Corn Exchange and Portland Hall. At this time it was a centre for reading sessions, plays and dances. The old machinery for corn hoisting was still in the attic part of the building, where old chests of deeds were also stored. By 1929, many buildings had changed, and shops had appeared on the ground floors. The white fronted building which was the first Price's School had given way to the Fire Station and shops were very much in evidence on the left hand side of the street.

What shops they were! Family owned, going through several generations, this was the time when you could depend upon a particular shop 'standing where it stood' for more than five years at a time. Neville's the chemist, Pullens, Olivers, Bishop's, Stead and Simpson's, all well known shoe shops; Croft's, a wonderful grocers, Boots the chemist, Phillips the dress shop, Letherens the drapery shop, Dodge's for dress and materials, which was to go on to celebrate its centenary; Sutton's the printers and bookshop, Silver's and Trigg's, both

lid view of West Street.

Portland Street.

tailors, and last, but not least in this short list, Batchelor's the chemist which was to remain a chemist for two hundred years.

We must not forget the family firm of Cripps the fishmonger and Jeffery's the furniture stores which are also in the area between the Wesleyan church and Westbury Manor.

There were also many smaller, essential retailing shops, Waters the fishmongers, Milbank's the butchers together with Burt's, another family butcher, Pyle's the bakers, Vimpany's, the jeweller and watchmakers, Millard's the corn merchants and Hayward's the greengrocers. (Apologies if I have not named your particular favourite — A.J.)

Dominating the left hand side was the building of Lloyds Bank once known as 'The Bank'. On the opposite side of the road, the old coachbuilding firm of Coles was now a car sales room and repair shop, to be associated with the name of Hinxman and thus carrying on a tradition from the time when coaches were built for George IV.

Cars were beginning to dominate the scene, parking in the middle of the road (as well as at the sides) starting the congestion in West Street which was particularly bad on Market Day. Nevertheless, it never seemed to bother anybody. Instead it was a happy, bustling street, never so crowded that friends and acquaintances could not meet nearly every time they went into town before wandering into Pyle's for coffee or lunch.

At the High Street end of West Street, there was still the Old Forge and Bennet and Righton's garage. Between many shops were spaces like Cawte's Place, open spaces which were used for allotments and gardens or led to a few cottages. Church Path, more generally known as 'Pyle's Alley', led directly across the road from Quay Street to the old Parish Church. Another led up by Barclays Bank to some old cottages which stood opposite some prefabricated buildings which were destined to become the 'Flying Angel' club, a parking place for ambulances and the first local municipal library. One well known droke or passage was (and still is) Adelaide passage. This led to a series of cottages with large gardens.

We must not forget that these were the days of few domestic refrigerators and other amenities now considered essential. Shopping was, therefore, often a daily affair and certainly afforded a chance of friendly meetings and a good gossip. The author remembers going into a grocer's shop during the height of summer to buy some bacon. The shopkeeper took the side of bacon and actually smelled it to ascertain that it was fit for sale. I am afraid his potential customer rejected it. There were, of course, no such things as frozen foods, chilled meals and sterile plastic wrappings. The milk arrived fresh, twice daily, and in the earlier part of this period was measured out, on the doorstep, into the housekeeper's own jug.

These were the days when radios were known as wireless sets, and most required a dry battery (H.T.) and a lead acid battery (accumulator). The latter would be collected by an errand boy who would provide a replacement whilst the other was being charged up.

Crofts – a wonderful grocers.
Below: The original forge with the path from West Street through to Quay Street.

Most shops sent around for orders and delivered the goods, often on the same day. So errand boys on their bikes, with the large baskets in front, were a common sight and usually a very cheerful one. How we miss their whistling of the latest popular song. We also miss the ice cream man on his tricycle (stop me and buy one!) — and the knife and scissors grinder — almost a part of the street furniture.

Before leaving West Street, do you remember — Messrs Dodge and Son?

Messrs Dodge and Son were destined to be one of the oldest firms in Fareham. An elderly resident of Fareham, talking about the firm where she and her family worked (her brother staying for fifty years), refers to the Dodge family as being the "kindliest people who ever lived; always a chair, a cup of tea and two biscuits for those who had walked in from the country."

It was a Working Person's Shop carrying anything needed in the way of boots and shoes, clothing and haberdashery. Their employees rarely left except to marry, and even then often returned to the firm after marriage. They did all they could to help their employees and put in to all departments overhead cash railways. These were a great joy to young and old. The money and bill were placed into a small wooden container and this was screwed to a wheeled lid which ran on the overhead wire from each counter to the cashier's desk. A lever was pulled and the little box was 'catapulted' along the wire (turning corners with a crash rather like a small version of a tramcar) to the cashier. She returned it with receipt and any change.

The author well remembers the delight with which her spaniel chased the little box to and fro, meanwhile sliding all over the polished linoleum, to the great amusement of all present and not excepting the manager, who used to stand waiting in anticipation.

Just after the Great War, men's suits, made on the premises, cost £3-10s (£3.50). Working shirts, cut out a dozen at a time by the manager, sold for 2/11 (about 15p). If something was, for example, 2/11¾, a packet of pins was given instead of the farthing change.

The shop was finally to close in 1970.

Opposite: Three views of West Street between the two World Wars.

The Fareham Fire Service into action in the early 1920s – shutting the horses into the wagon shafts.

Now they are off!

The Fire Service

When dealing with the Fire Station, we are fortunate that Mr. Arthur Sutton kept a scrap book of everything dealing with the fire service from about 1906. Problems of horses, securing of new platforms, desire for new fire engines, competitions, actual fires, and confrontations with the Council (who hated spending money) are all recorded. Mr. Sutton, a printer and bookseller by trade, was a devoted member and staunch leader of the Fire Service. True, he demanded a 'gold' helmet, when the rest had 'silver' ones. Surely this was so that he might be more quickly recognised at a fire. True also, he expected the fire engine to be diverted to pick him up if there was a fire — but these are small quibbles.

If Mr. Sutton happened to be 'missing' from a fire, it was through ill health and this was duly recorded in the newspaper. He served for fifty years, over a period when reading the extracts one is amazed at the risks which had to be taken and were undertaken willingly.

Distances undertaken were great, especially considering that horse-drawn transport was still commonplace well after the Great War. Fareham went to fires as far afield as Bridgemary, Lee on the Solent, Crofton, Wickham and Droxford. Small wonder that the fire was sometimes out or a building had been totally destroyed before they got there.

Problems with the Council are shown in struggles to secure a new platform for practising, a new fire station, a new steamer and a motor fire engine. Most of these matters were not decided under three years. For example, protests at the buying of a new platform were voiced by a councillor who claimed they were being asked to pay £6 for a chute when they had just sold one to the senior boys' school for £3. He said "Just to protect the lives of a few boys when there were 6,000 people to protect in Fareham."

Prior to the 1914 war, Fareham's 'new' Fire Station in West Street had been built on the site of the old Price's School. The Fire Brigade had also acquired a steamer but the horses were kept in a field some distance away. As problems arose during the Great War, Mr. Fred Dyke, who was destined to become a leading business man, stepped in, offering to provide horses and a field close by.

Shortly after the war, starting in 1919, a demand arose for a motor fire engine. But for four more years, the Brigade had to make do with horses. The debate to-ed and fro-ed both across the Council Chamber and with the Fire Brigade. "The horsedrawn one was good enough . . . a motor fire engine wouldn't be satisfactory over rough ground . . . But what about the distances that had to be covered? . . . What about the *cost*?"

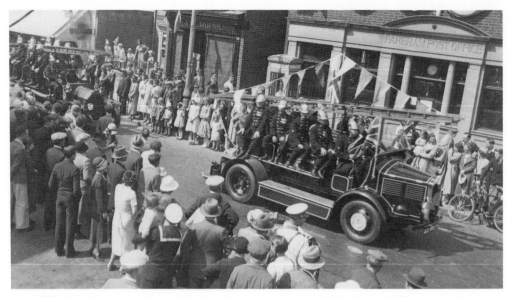

The Fareham Brigade – with their fire engine in the 1935 Silver Jubilee procession.

At last, in 1923, the Brigade got their motor engine at the cost of £800, and a telegram from Messrs Dennis Bros. advised of its readiness and invited "someone to go up and have a joy-ride back".

Early fires at Wicor Bone Works and as far afield as Swanwick and the King's Head Hotel at Wickham fully justified the purchase. In 1929, a trailer was bought just in time to go into action at two serious fires at Wickham and others at Forton and Swanwick.

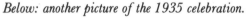

Below: another picture of the 1935 celebration.

On parade again. This time for the Coronation of 1937.

The Silver Jubilee of King George V (1935) was duly celebrated with a procession through the town and led by an extra new fire engine. All too soon, in 1937, was to come the coronation of George VI. It was, of course, celebrated by a Church Parade, and the inevitable procession took place — equally inevitably, partially ruined by thunder and torrential rain.

By now the war clouds were gathering, and in 1937, Air Raid Precautions (ARP) were being planned and volunteers were being asked for. Fareham required 520 men and 200 women.

Arthur Sutton officially retired as Chief Fire Officer in 1938, but not until after he had coped with two huge fires — one at the Meon Valley Timber Yard where the Fareham Fire Brigade was joined by four other brigades and the fire was fought for forty-eight hours; the other at Down End House where great damage was done to an attractive Georgian mansion. In November, Mr. Sutton celebrated his retirement at the Annual Fire Brigade Supper. In his speech he recalled the time when the 'escape' was fitted with a chute — "During the demonstration, one of the firemen caught his helmet in the chute and remained suspended inside for several minutes before being rescued."

31

At the Fareham Fire Brigade Annual Dinner in 1939, Arthur Sutton received a silver salver and cheque from the Rt. Hon. Sir Thomas Inskip, the guest speaker. Five toasts (at least that number was recorded!) were drunk and entertainment was provided by the Southsea Singers, Mr. Bert Chant (entertainer) and Mr. Cochrane on the piano accordion. This was the last happy re-union before the Second World War started, but at least before then, Fareham got another new fire engine!

The Market

There has long been a market in Fareham. An old document shows that a public meeting to establish a market in Fareham was held in 1795 and that the first market, to be continued every fortnight subsequently, was conducted on Monday, April 22nd, 1795.

It is entirely probable that there was in fact an unofficial market before this. The old Market House, later known as Howards House, stood at the end of a row of houses in the middle of West Street, conveniently close to the old Parish Pump and the Cage or Lock-up. Thus the keepers of law and order were well prepared for most contingencies (though not, however, for the time when somebody went off with the key to the Cage and a plea was made for its return!) and for many years there must have been problems for, after all, there were at least eight pubs in the vicinity, all doing a roaring trade on market day. This roaring trade had not ceased by the time of the Second World War!

The animals, usually cattle, sheep and pigs, were increasingly being brought in by train and lorries in the 1930s, although many were still driven in 'on the hoof' the day before and kept overnight in fields and pounds mainly to the north of the town. They were then driven through the streets into West Street and were paraded in front of the Fire Station which was near the Parish Pump. They caused complete chaos to traffic and complaints inevitably grew, until in about 1920, they were stalled immediately in the market place. A Market Company, founded at the end of the previous century, had purchased land which was to become the market place. It was controlled by Austin and Wyatt.

Even so, the animals were still driven through the streets and this lasted well into the Second World War years. Woe betide anyone who worked in Portsmouth if they did not catch an earlier bus on Mondays.

Probably the last true drover connected with Fareham was Bill Hiscock. A small man, never without his stick and dog, he always wore heavy hobnailed boots, corduroy trousers held up below the knee with string and sported a red and white spotted handkerchief. When in Fareham, he always lodged overnight at No. 2, Russell Place Cottages, off Trinity Street. Another man who should be mentioned, although we stray into the Second World War years, was Jack Anderson who worked for Knowle Hospital Farm. He walked the four miles to market, with a bull on the end of a 'bull pole'. This was a six feet long pole with a clip at one end to clip onto the ring in the bull's nose. It was a wonderful effort.

To many residents, Monday market was a great delight for there were also chickens, ducks and geese, rabbits, sometimes puppies and also farm produce.

To one resident it was even more exciting "if an animal escaped in West Street". This was not an unusual occurrence although perhaps few were as exciting as one in the 1930s, when a bull broke loose to do the round trip of Fareham by charging down Quay Street, across the recreation ground, up Bath Lane, along West Street and into Kings Road and the allotments where it was finally put out of its misery. Another bullock broke out of Breton's, a butcher then at the corner of Trinity Street, and was chased along West Street to the Gillies and into the stonemason's yard where it was caught. Perhaps less exciting, but more chaotic, was the arrival of a loose animal in one of the shops in West Street. Everybody out!

Farmers hung over the stalls and assessed the stock before auction whilst sightseers looked on. There was much absenteeism from school on Mondays and a wary eye was always kept out for the Truancy Officer. After the market the farmers adjourned to the pubs, where much extra business was transacted. Meanwhile the animals could be driven on the hoof to the railway station or even to the central abattoir in Portsmouth. Alternatively they went to the local butchers for slaughtering (hence the butchers were closed on Mondays) and others were either driven or transported to their new farms.

As time went on, trade in the market place grew more mixed with flowers, fruit and vegetables and even clothes and crockery for sale.

An early picture of sheep in West Street being driven from the market.

The Fareham market.

Some concluding memories from Mr. Swinburne, of Austin and Wyatt. Up to the 1940s the Fareham and Hants Farmers Club ran a stallion. The groom and stallion called periodically at the Fareham office for instructions: all the staff at the Fareham office were obliged to form the labour force at the Fareham and Hants Farmers Club's Show every Whit Monday and finally, staff working after 7 p.m. on settling the Fareham Market accounts were paid sixpence (two and a half pence in today's currency) tea money!

The Red Lion — and Florence White

The Red Lion.

The Red Lion was one of the great coaching inns, containing an 18th century minstrels gallery, still unspoilt at the beginning of World War Two. It was an important centre for public and private dinners, dances and Hunt Balls. A one time resident of High Street says "The Sailing Club dances were the high spot of the winter. The floor, a little uneven, was polished with beeswax, but beautifully smooth."

Associated with the Red Lion was Florence White, an important cookery expert. She had been on long visits to the Red Lion from 1870 onwards, as she had three maiden aunts who owned the hotel. Her interest in cookery grew and right up to the 1930s she was writing cookery articles in the press and in magazines.

In 1932, Florence White published a book of *Real English Cookery*, which the *Times* newspaper described as 'one of the most romantic cookery books ever written'.

In 1936, she took possession of 160 West Street as a 'House of Studies'. This was to be the Headquarters of the English Folk Cooking Association. She stated "At the House there is no distinction of classes; Admirals' wives, Colonels' daughters, daughters of unemployed miners and other girls who earned their living in different ways as cooks, kitchen maids etc., all worked together side by side without any trace of snobbery in anyone. Each student makes her own place in everyone's estimation according to her personal character and disposition. A farm worker's daughter may be as well bred as the daughter of a duchess, sometimes better.

"I chose Fareham as the headquarters because my aunts had kept the Red Lion Hotel and Assembly Rooms. It was from then on that I learnt the good epicurean country house cookery which had been handed down in the family since the days of Queen Elizabeth. Many of the recipes, I have been able to trace through historical and literary research."

Sadly, by 1938 the premises were beginning to look neglected and devoid of activity and her rates were in arrears. She promised to pay off at least some of the arrears when she received fees for articles she was writing. As time went on, her position became worse and by the end of 1939 she had no source of income. She was over ninety years of age, her failing sight had turned to total blindness and she became one of those few pathetic souls whose rates were excused on the grounds of poverty. She just disappeared from the scene. The sad end of a most distinguished person.

Writing of Florence White leads us naturally from West Street and the Red Lion into High Street, for Florence had returned to Fareham to take care of her aunts when they lived at 79, High Street, near its junction with Union Street.

A panoramic view of one of Br

High Street

At the bottom of High Street is a triangular shaped island of buildings and houses. Between the world wars it was the site of the home of Mr. Edney with its gardens and with the corn merchant's shop next door. Austin and Wyatt were, and still are, on the corner but the other buildings of that time have now given way to photographers and opticians.

Union Street, marking one side of the triangle, was so named because of the first Union Workhouse. The small street had contained three pubs or ale houses — the White Lion which was still in existence in the early 1930s and appears to have had quite a large brewhouse; the Robin Hood and Little John and the Blacksmith's Arms.

High Street, like many of the older streets of Fareham, is numbered consecutively, up the left hand side going north and back down the right hand side.

These days, it seems incredible to think that in the 1950s, a small band of 'conservationists' had to get together to save High Street from development. David Lloyd was to describe it as "One of the most attractive country town High Streets in southern England".

38

Georgian High Streets.

It has also been called one of the finest Georgian High Streets. In fact, the buildings are an attractive mixture of styles and period, some being even disguised Tudor. Between some of the larger houses were passages leading to 'courts' of cottages.

High Street changed little between the wars. There were a few scattered shops, mainly near West Street, but High Street was in general, residential. The trees on the right hand side of the road, once actually stood in the road but kerb stones were put along the front and the space filled in with cobbles. This had been part of the site of the important old Cheese Fair.

No. 1 High Street, was for many years a draper's shop belonging to Mr. Warn, who was well known not only for his shop but also for his 'falsetto' voice in the Fareham Male Voice Choir. He also created interest about town by riding on a Dursley Pederson Bicycle — a bike which had a net hammock and cushion slung between what would be the modern seat pillar and handlebars.

Next were the Fareham Cycle Works (Fareham was rich in cycle works having had a Cycling Club in the late 19th century). Again illustrations show that the street had not really changed for nearly eighty years. In the 1930s Mr. May had taken over the cycle agency and the Rosemary Tea Rooms had arrived. The well known firm of Abraham, noted for their furnishings and furniture, came next. Tragedy overcame this family in 1926 and the business was taken over by Pitchers. Cooper's, at No. 4, was an important wholesale tobacco agent.

39

High Street.

. . . and still High Street.

Duffett's, the printers, was in one of the courts joined to High Street by a short passage, as was Jno Croad, the builders at 6a. Their court was particularly attractive. No. 7, in 1930 the home of Lt. Commander Everett, has always been reputed to be haunted.

Whilst No. 12's claim to fame was that for several years it was occupied by the mother of Arthur Lee, M.P. for South Hants. He was to become Lord Lee of Fareham and between the wars presented his celebrated house, 'Chequers,' to the nation as a country home for the Prime Minister.

No. 21, occupied in 1930 by Mr. Papillon, owes its fame to having been the birthplace of Sir John Goss. He was to become organist of the Chapel Royal and St. Paul's Cathedral.

Before reaching the Golden Lion, we would pass yet another cycle dealer and three Elizabethan cottages with a passage leading to more at the back. From here, the road starts to slope down hill, an old sweet shop stood here and yet another motor and cycle makers, this time, Hansford's. The road here was known as Vicar's Hill, the name still commemorated on a house wall. A few cottages built sideways to the road marked Church Place and led directly to a pair of the Parish Church gates. They were, in fact, exactly opposite the old Vicarage. A cluster of buildings bordered the bottom of High Street opposite the old Post Office.

Crossing the road, it was impossible not to notice Wallington Hill, a trial in its steepness to pedestrians, cyclists and motorists alike — as it had been to horse-drawn coaches in the past and was destined to be for learner drivers in the future!

On this side of the road we find the fine houses with the large gardens stretching right down to the river Wallington and the Old Mill Pond. The tidal waters reached much further before the Second World War when there was much silting and there was frequent flooding at the bottom of the gardens. There seems to be no doubt that in years passed some smuggling went on. Big houses included Wallington Hill House and Lysses House. The Old Vicarage was reputed to have a passage underground coming out at the Church and certainly a blocked up doorway was found (although it was not explored).

In 1939, Rev. Tarbat's son was to write his recollections of Fareham. He used the name 'Upmarket' for Fareham and called himself Cecil Dundon. Well known people were mentioned and a fine time was had by all endeavouring to recognise people and places mentioned under pseudonyms. It is really a fascinating and amusing book.

Next to Collins the butchers are several old cottages. The first one was occupied by Mrs. Russell, who, in 1931, was stated to be the oldest woman in England and was destined to reach the age of 107. The newspapers annually recorded her age and her photograph appeared, also annually with an advertisement for Carters Little Liver Pills!

Vicar's Hill

Pyle's bakery made wonderful birthday cakes for her and exhibited them in their shop. At the age of 104 her picture was in the paper and showed the cake carrying 104 candles. The article stated that "She spent a happy birthday, receiving many visitors and eighty presents. The visitors were impressed both by her cheerfulness and mental alertness. She was asked her opinion of the short skirts now being worn (1931) and replied with warm emphasis "they would not suit me at all!'.''

The big house called Rose Neath was once the home of the Stewards of Cams Hall and speaking tubes led through to the adjoining cottages. Further down the street, Lysses Path was yet another passage, this time leading straight to East Street and a bridge over the river. Surrounding it were gardens and market gardens. Unfortunately, smuggling tales come outside the scope of this period, but collapsed passages and ground subsidences probably tell their own story. Between No. 67 and the County Club there is yet another passage which can be closed by huge gates and led to more gardens and allotments. The County Club is pure Georgian, now over 200 years old.

In 1928, a girls' private school moved from Western House in West Street to Wykeham House, 69 High Street, where it was to remain for 60 years. The Headmistress was Miss Alsop. She retired in 1937 to be succeeded briefly by Mr. and Mrs. Cross. The school deteriorated to 37 pupils, but in 1939 it was taken over by Mrs. Duff and Miss Beer and numbers rose rapidly. No. 67 later became part of the school.

Kintyre House sits back from the road. This fine house with its magnificent porch was occupied between the wars by Admiral Donaldson, a law unto himself. Should a car be parked in front of his house even for a short time, he would telephone the police to have it removed.

'Butterwicks', Park Lane before the development of the Uplands Estate.

'The Potteries', the home of Mr. J. Sandy, a local pottery owner.

Still Near The Town Centre

Although Fareham extended relatively little outwards between the wars, there had been and was a considerable amount of what would now be called 'in-filling'. Old Fareham had a positive warren of passages, courts and yards often containing many cottages and leading from the more important streets. They were often places of great poverty. But roads and lanes were being developed. Osborn Road had been developed for large houses before the Great War, as had Portland Street, Hartlands Road (once Blind Lane) and Southampton Road. Roads and lanes being developed included New Road (which quickly lost its former name of Nightingale Lane), Colenso Road, School Road (soon to become Gordon Road) and Grove Road.

In 1927 there was another significant development when it was planned to develop the land between Old Turnpike and Park Lane. It was meant to be a complete 'pear-shaped' estate, but a later developer extended Serpentine Road to come out at Park Lane and thus cut off the end of Harrison Road. Uplands Crescent was also started. A plan to develop Osborn Road through to Trinity Street and beyond was blocked by a Captain Miller.

He had come to live at Northwood, which lies to the east of Park Lane and when 'Uplands' came on the market, he bought the estate. It was his hope to keep the open country southwards from 'Uplands'. He sold the extreme south of the estate (which still contains the South Lodge) to the Council on condition that it was to be a recreation ground. The large open fields with the pond and trees were a joy for walkers and children as well as providing a short cut to Red Barns Lane and Fontley. He did offer the land between the recreation ground and 'Uplands' to Price's School governors for £2,000. They turned it down!

Trinity Street, a relatively short street with its old cottages and Bastard Lane and Place, now more genteelly known as Russell Lane and Place, was fortunate in having four public houses. True, the Royal Oak was on the corner with West Street but there was also the Good Intent, the Victory and the Sun. The latter was an old, small pub and was once considered the 'home from home' of some of the masters from Price's School.

Standing endways to Park Lane was 'Butterwicks' (a much older building than 'Uplands'), which had eight large rooms with bathroom and kitchen and a large lean-to. It was possibly the earlier farm house for the estate or even a country house. At various times, as the ground was dug in the adjoining park, foundations and remains of walls were discovered in several places. In one, some thirty square feet of a brick floor were discovered about 18 inches under the surface and during a dry summer a large patch of dead grass indicated another foundation under the front lawn. Two more floors were found and also two wells and a wet season uncovered yet another floor. Paved tracks were uncovered in the plantation to the north.

For a time, the house was divided into two, but in the 1930s it was again made into one house. Inside the panelling of one of the staircases removed at this time, the following was found, written in pencil on the insides of the boards: '1814 bread 3d a loaf, 1815 bread 11d a loaf. What is a poor man to do? W. Robinson.'

Sadly no excavations were done before the cottage was destroyed, although the late Mr. J. P. Garrad did find a small treasure trove while digging in his garden in 1936. Had there, he wondered, perhaps been a highwayman living there once?

The upper part of Park Lane was tree-lined, with open fields which were often occupied overnight by animals due to be driven to the market on Monday. It was to remain like this for years.

From here we find the old brickfields and clay pits, the oldest of which were already being used for housing developments. On the land between Wickham Road and Old Turnpike stood 'The Potteries', a large house standing on five acres of old clay pit. It was owned by Mr. J. Sandy, a local pottery owner. The garden, terraced to make use of the various levels of clay cutting, was magnificent. The house still stands but modern building occupies the old garden.

Meanwhile, to the south of the town, the large Belvoir House, facing the Town Quay, was demolished in the early 1930s, and another estate was going up. The original houses of Belvoir Close lie above the level of the road with the estate wall marking their boundaries. The house had two lodges, one of which still remains. Houses were also to extend along the Gosport Road although the big house, 'Southfields', with its large gardens was still in occupation. Cams Alders farm was to be taken over by Tom Parker's Dairies and his fleet of horse-drawn milk floats were a common sight in Fareham. Those horses knew their own rounds and heaven help the milkman who delayed too long for the horse would just set off. Elsewhere were open fields, but Redlands Lane, which originally had only two buildings, Minden Cottages and Allders Farm, was to lose these in the 1920s for the development of the Redlands Estate.

We have already mentioned 'Redlands' and 'Bishopswood' at the entrance to Redlands Lane. After the Paxton Road development came Allders Farm, destined to be pulled down in the 1920s. Its lands extended from Redlands Lane through to the railway line and it had good cattle grazing lands with long gardens attached to the two cottages of the farm workers. The Gilly or Blackbrook wound through its valley known as the Gillies, eventually coming out at Fareham Creek. At this time it was tidal, the lower part could be flooded and the water quite deep. In the Gillies were allotments, rented out for 2/6d (12½p) a year.

Belvoir House – and (below) Tom Parker's fleet of milk carts.

47

On the opposite side of the road, the fields stretching through to Stubbington were marshy and could be under water in winter. No wonder the area was once described as "one of the best snipe shooting regions of the country".

There was always a gypsy encampment in Redlands Lane, still commemorated by a small pathway known as Gypsy Lane. The family on the encampment were ruled by a rod of iron, by a Matriarch and Gypsy Queen — Mrs. Birch. They were a well respected family in Fareham.

Strawberry fields extended on either side of a path which led eventually to Burnt House Lane, Stubbington. Extending from the Gillies up to Mill Road were the fields belonging to Coombe Farm.

Walking north, west or east along any of these roads, open country and farm lands were quickly reached. There were so many farms, Furze Hill, Hellyers, Dean, Charity, Heytesbury, Albany, North Fareham and Crocker Hill leading towards Wickham; Red Barn, Brook Farm and Blackbrook going westwards and White Dell, Spurlings, East Cams, Cams Home Farm, Down End and Down Barn Farm on the other side of Fareham, all combined to make Fareham and its market thrive.

Trinity Street on King George V's Silver Jubilee, 1935.

When Mr. and Mrs. Wylde, of Fontley, went for a cycle ride up Park Lane on their honeymoon they were stopped by a photographer – to be caught on a picture post card forever! Below: also in Park Lane – clearing up fallen trees after the great storm of 1933.

Mr. Mills who had an acre of land behind Staceys (in his greenhouse in 1963).

Small wonder that the words of William Cobbett, written a hundred years previously, still applied, "Miles of corn fields, the land is excellent and the spot the earliest in the whole Kingdom. Here the first sheaf is cut that is cut in England, that the reader may depend upon . . . the wheat as good if not rather better than on the South Downs, and the barley as good as it is possible to be."

Market gardening and allotment holdings were always important. One remembers Mr. Collins of Adelaide Place, Mr. Coker with his vegetable cart, Mr. Drover of Trinity Street famed for his chrysanthemums and Mr. Mills with his acre of land lying behind Staceys in West Street.

Strawberries were not widely grown locally, the most important area being around the present Oak Road. But they were brought in from Titchfield, Sarisbury, Swanwick and Wickham (to name but four centres) in rail vans to be marshalled at Fareham station and from where two trains carrying strawberries left daily. Mr. A. Swatton, at that time about 15 years of age, used to have to load up the shelves in the special vans and if they ran out of vans, old carriages were used and the baskets stacked on the floors.

Leading To The Port

Three roads led from the town to the Port of Fareham. Quay Street (once South Street) is the oldest. In 1930, it had three corn merchants with big warehouses and had contained several passages and yards. Those nearer the quay had largely disappeared leaving two cottages set back near the viaduct and a small group of cottages which curved round the corner to the Upper Wharf. Cripps, the fishmongers, was at No. 10 in 1930, and Fareham Urban District Council offices were at No. 21, an imposing Georgian house, later to be the Register Office. The original telephone exchange was to become Clack's general store, the *Portsmouth Evening News* office was at No. 25 and one important old yard sat sideways onto the road. This was Clarke's Yard.

Quay Street.

When Millards were converting cottages into a shop in Quay Street, it was found to have a subterranean passage and a secret hiding place. What was thought to be a well in the kitchen was discovered to be the start of an underground passage leading to the creek. The second discovery was a small staircase hidden beside a chimney and leading to an attic hide-away. Coins dating back to 1729 were found under the floorboards.

Mr. George Privett was consulted and believed that the passage and cottage were most probably associated with smuggling activities in Quay Street and linked to an old beer house known as 'The Drum and Monkey'. Smuggled goods were kept in Hewlett's Yard and the cottages must have been particularly useful as the Customs were at the 'Chequers' public house almost just across the road.

There was for many years a large open space by Holy Trinity Church. This was a cricket field and space for fetes, fairs, circuses and the annual fireworks. It was lost after the Great War by the building of Kings, Queens and Western roads and by the building housing the Territorial Army. Part of the original space still remained in front of this building leading to Hartlands Road, once known as Blind Lane.

Hartlands Road was mainly residential in character. One side of the road was occupied by the gardens of Westbury Manor, reaching down almost to the Roman Catholic church. The other side of the road did have a builders' merchant and several older cottages before the viaduct was reached. Once again we are led to the Quay and the junction with Portland Street and Quay Street.

Portland Street was destined to have the shortest life of the three. It is now (1989) being pulled down and will have lasted just over 100 years. Now that part of the bus station area has *again* been pulled down (remember the cottages on the corner?), the name of Solomon, the corn merchant, has been revealed on the wall.

Portland Street was a busy street. Traffic, of course, travelled in both directions and there was a tramway to add to the confusion. A tram ride was very bumpy. It could also be exciting as when a tram collided with a fire steamer under the viaduct! It gave a feeling of superiority when it was possible to travel freely in a tram, while the rest of the traffic was held up, at times such as Fleet Reviews or when the Schneider Trophy Race was being held.

The street possessed a wine merchants — Clacks', and a Beer retailer; these were destined to become the Portland Arms and the Toby Jug. Interspersed with houses in the 1930s were Cooper's the confectioners, Mr. Evans at the bakery, who made his bread using faggots of wood for his oven, and yet another bootmaker, Jackson's. Near the bottom of the street was the Presbytery of the Roman Catholic church, while at the bottom on the opposite side was Irvine Haley, the timber merchant. Fred Dyke had a blacksmith's shop at No. 34.

The Register Office in Quay Street.

Quay Street before alterations showing the old mill storage, Georgian houses, Millards and Clacks' store – once the telephone exchange.

Top of Portland Street.

He was steadily making his way up in the world, from horse and cart and rented barges to a place on the Council and sufficient land and horses to assist the Fire Brigade. His haulage business grew steadily and he established an office and garages actually under the viaduct arches.

With Portland Street and two other roads converging onto the Gosport Road there were perpetual traffic problems. Time and again the roads were changed, islands and kerbs appeared and disappeared, Burrell's fountain was removed, a raised rose garden was planted and was finally removed to create a new alignment "so that traffic might flow more easily under the viaduct". Judge the amusement when the making of the new road revealed the old tram lines!

Below: The Presbytery and the R.C. church in Portland Street.

The Eastern End

It is when we follow the old roads that we begin to see how important was the Port of Fareham with its many quays for shipping, its mills and its boatbuilding and ancillary industries. We can prove this yet again by re-starting at the Red Lion Hotel and walking eastwards. Having passed Russell Place and Lusby's Provision Stores we find several large Georgian houses. These include Burpham House which lies near Bath Lane. Bath Lane has changed its name three times. Initially it was Park Lane but in Victorian times, two bathing houses were built on the local quay, so the road became Bathing House Lane. With the end of the bathing houses the name was shortened to Bath Lane.

The Georgian houses are to be found on both sides of the road. A special mention should be made of Fareham House set sideways on to the road, once the home of generations of the Loring family connected with the Royal Navy, for a time the home of Sir Roger Keyes and in the 1930s the home of Doctor Stevenson. Fairfield House, with its magnificent grounds and gardens, was pulled down and the piggeries became Cedar Cottage and later Cedar Cafe. From there the road slopes steeply towards the river and the Mill Pond, to be joined at the bottom by Lysses Path.

The eastern entrance to West Street.

-55·

Fareham House.

Fairfield House was pulled down but its piggeries later became Cedar Cottage (seen here) and later still Cedar Cafe.

East Street.

Cams Hill – it was like this in the 1920s.

Bridg

It was at Bridgefoot that much of village life and activity took place. The Pond was deep and tidal and the road from East Street was steep with a sharp turn at the bottom. This frequently proved disastrous for carts and motorists who often headed straight into the water. The road then crossed the outfalls from the Mill Pond by a rather hump-backed bridge and passed under the viaduct. The remains of the old tidal mill were on the right and the road then made another sharp angled turn to climb Cams Hill, passing the Delme Arms on the left.

It was well after the Second World War that the new road to Portsmouth was put through, and before that travel by bus on a winter's morning could prove a little complicated. The buses could not get up Cams Hill and passengers ended up by walking up the hill to be met by another bus to take them on their way.

But let us return to Bridgefoot and follow the coast back to the main port. We find the remains of a stone quay right by the outfalls of the Mill Pond as ships carrying grain came up as far as here. In fact, it was possible for special small barges to go through to quays in Wallington. Also starting at Bridgefoot was an attractive drive known as the Esplanade, which was wide enough for two carriages and was a popular walk. Unfortunately the Mill Pond was gradually silting up, the silt and marsh gaining control and the Esplanade began to break down. By the end of the Second World War further deterioration had set in and there certainly would not have been room for even one carriage and pair.

ham.

The Esplanade passed Bathing House Quay, later to become Gas House Quay and from here crossing Bath Lane the town recreation ground was reached.

The Mill Pond.

Esplanade Bridgefoot, Fareham   PN1450

Two views of Bridgefoot – below: the Esplanade. In this picture of the Recreation Ground are Payne's cottages by the creek.

Recreation Ground. Fareham.

Around The Quay

The Recreation Ground was given to the people of Fareham in the 19th century and, therefore, unlike many parks and playing grounds has never been locked up at night. There was some attempt to charge entrance fees by some of the Societies and Clubs, but the 'Ferrumites' would have nothing of it. They were quite correct.

For many years, Payne's Cottages and their gardens, together with a well, stood between the recreation ground and the water's edge. There were railings around for safety but few children could resist the temptation to pull themselves up on the railings to try to look down the well! Eventually the cottages were pulled down and the rough land was added to the recreation ground.

The white yacht seen in the foreground of the panoramic picture, was in fact Fareham's only steam yacht and belonged to Dr. Woakes, of Belvoir House. When fully in commission it made a brave sight with its brass, bell-mouthed, brightly polished funnel.

Apart from being used for sports and a general playing area, the grounds were also the scene of Fire Brigade practices and demonstrations. In the middle of one of these, in 1925, the display was abandoned when a fire alert was raised for a fire on an old German U-boat, moored near the Upper Wharf. Oil from it had also caught fire and it took two hours to bring everything under control.

We must not forget Mr. Wassell. Generally known as 'Fiery' Wassell, he was for many years a pilot on the river, and in his spare time rowed people out to their boats or across the creek to Cams for a ½d. After the Great War, four U-boats were brought up the creek to be scrapped. They included the one which sank the Lusitania. One was complete — the UC 9 which was open to visitors at the cost of 3d a time. As the U-boats remained moored for so many years, it was inevitable that children were liable to sneak on to play. Fiery Wassell was the pilot who guided these U-boats up the river, and I am afraid that he was quietly referred to, by the youngsters, as Herr Von Wassell. He died in 1925.

There was to be little change in the region around the Upper Wharf for many years. There was an outcry when the wharf was enclosed by Fraser and White who took over the large Georgian house, and as a concession two of the railings were made moveable so that access was possible. We must remember that this was still an important bathing area and we have a delightful picture taken in 1933 of children lined up in the water. The Upper Wharf area, which now links us up with Quay Street, was a hive of activity. Coal was brought in by ship and barge to be sorted and marketed. There were ships of all ages

A panorami

moored at the various quays and the craft of boat building in Fareham goes back many centuries. At the Upper Wharf, the boat building yard of R. and A. Hamper dates from 1926 and boats could and can still be seen being built and launched down a small slipway. The firm also had a boatyard in Mill Lane and the men used to haul the hulls down to the Upper Wharf. At this point Fraser and White's disconnected the buckets from their cranes and using the 'grabs' from the cranes, swung the boats across and into the water.

The Town Quay extended all along the Gosport Road and ships were moored side by side out into the Creek. Grain, timber, bricks and tiles were manhandled across. At high water it was common for the road by the Town Quay to be flooded and this also occurred at the slipway at the Lower Quay. Belvoir House, across the road from the Quay was on higher ground. It was pulled down in the 1930s and Belvoir Close was built in its place. The house 'Elmhurst' was to remain, as was Lakeside House. The latter flanked the Gillies and was found to have been built originally as two cottages. The cellar walls were made of ballast stones. Close by, and conveniently placed, was Bellamy's forge.

Two public houses nearby ministered to the needs of shore workers and sailors — the Coal Exchange and the Castle in the Air. A short distance up the hill were the Rising Sun and the Bird in Hand (the latter's sign says 'A bird in hand far better 'tis, than two that in the bushes is!').

THE QUAY, FAREHAM

e Quay.

The Lower Quay was always busy and as the river began to silt up, larger ships made use of it. They brought into the area coal, timber from Scandinavia, stone from Portland and granite and gravel. In the past, fine ironwork had

'Fiery' Wassell, skilled river pilot.

been sent to the naval dockyard at Portsmouth from Fontley Iron Mills. Tiles, chimney pots, agricultural products and especially Fareham Red bricks were exported, the latter ending up all over the world. On the Lower Quay itself was a corrugated iron hut belonging to the owners of Down End Quarry, who shipped whitening on a schooner destined for the River Mersey. From here it went by barges to Wedgwood's Potteries.

Also on the wharf was the Fareham Flour Mill, run at this time by the Heasman family. It did a thriving trade and was noted for its loyal workforce.

The big houses, 'Southfields' and Prospect House, were nearby, and behind them were market gardens, land and cottages owned by the Adams family.

Many derelict hulks (including submarines) were towed upstream from Portsmouth, usually to rust away; but there were also houseboats, yachts and boats belonging to the Sea Scouts and the Fareham Sailing Club. Their club boat got the nickname of 'Watahole'. The creek was the centre for yachting and yacht races right through from Victorian times.

Yachting started up again after the Great War and Mr. J. P. Garrad in his 'History of the Sailing Club' tells some delightful yarns. One set of races was to have an hilarious ending. Caught part way down the creek in a force eight

The Upper Quay.

Some of the staff of the Fareham Flour Mills Co. Ltd. with Mr. Hilton Heasman sitting in the centre, flanked by Mr. Schmidt (foreman) and Mr. Richards (secretary).

Bathing at the Quay.

gust and unable to haul in spinnakers, the yachts headed steadily towards and finally through the reed beds and onto the mudflats. For many days after, the owners could be seen digging channels through the mud to get their boats out.

Lower down the harbour, Mr. Percy See was building fast sailing boats, cabin cruisers, naval rescue craft and speedboats. The latter were his pride and joy. He was the first man to put compasses in speedboats, a fortunate development as previously five speedboats had set off in a race for France. After several hours, one fetched up on the coast and the crew, having greeted the inhabitants in their best schoolboy French were answered in good Essex dialect! Mr. See was to build for the Hon. Mrs. Victor Bruce a speedboat which was to do a double cross channel trip in under two hours.

The creek was also the centre for the annual Aquatic Games and Regatta. These involved straightforward sailing races, rowing races including separate races for girls and women and costume races. There were swimming and diving competitions. Less serious were the two Greasy Pole competitions held in front of the Flour Mill. The vertical pole had a leg of pork or mutton at the top as a prize, the horizontal pole extended over the water and also had a prize at the end of it. Many inadvertent bathes took place.

A highlight was always the Duck Hunt. The 'duck' usually an excellent swimmer and diver often had to be co-opted for the event. The 'hunters' sat in ordinary galvanised bathtubs and paddles with garden shovels. The hunt ended when all the hunters were sunk. The aim of the 'hunter' was to paddle alongside the 'duck' and pat him on the head, which would make the 'hunter' the winner. This seldom happened. As the 'hunter' neared the 'duck' it disappeared below the surface and all watched breathlessly, guessing what was going to happen. A head appeared behind or on the opposite side of the 'hunter', a hand shot out, grasped the side of the bath, 'hunter' and spade went overboard and the bath sank. At low tide next day the 'hunters' were to be seen paddling over the mudbanks to recover their baths and shovels!

The events finished in the late evening. There were processions of decorated and illuminated boats and festivities were completed with a huge bonfire and fireworks on Cams Point.

In 1938, a successful and interesting experiment was carried out. With the exceptional high tide due, five dinghies sailed up the creek and got through the tunnel under the bridge by the overflow channels at Bridgefoot and into the Mill Pond. In spite of the growth of marsh they were able to row to within sight of Wallington Bridge, thus proving that barges were once able to sail to the quays at Wallington. On their return and with the rising tide, they had to lie flat on their backs in their dinghies and propel themselves through the tunnel by working their hands on its roof.

Below: The Gosport and Fareham Tramways power station (later to be pulled down and replaced by a laundry) was built on an old Royal Naval graveyard at the Lower Quay.

Damming The Creek

From time to time over the years, one particular 'coat-tail' has been trailed in Fareham. This is the recurring idea of damming the Mill Pond or the Creek.

A good example was in 1934 and is chronicled in a series of letters in a local paper. Someone, whose pen name was 'Lover of Fareham', suggested that it was time Fareham woke up and thought there should be a dam across the Creek. In reply, J.P.G. wrote to say the matter had been raised a few years previously and he hoped it had sunk into oblivion. He was against it; there was the problem of sewage outfall, the fact that unless there was a lock, boats would only be able to sail round and round in circles, that the lake, at first salty, would be receiving water from the river Wallington, and would be turned into near freshwater encouraging mosquitoes. All this, together with the capital outlay, the cost of a lock keeper, the problems for shipping and the fact that the Admiralty had foreshore rights made the plan unfeasible. After this devastating letter he retired from the fray.

'Alders Road' thought the dam was a good idea and thought that perhaps one correspondent enjoyed seeing old bedsteads, pots and pans, and motor tyres which "seemed to have a habit of finding their way into the creek overnight". Side tracking (as seems to be the habit in local affairs) he thought Fareham needed a hospital, a clinic and a public library.

On the same day, W.J.R. took a swipe at an earlier correspondent, suggesting that he must be new to the area and must like the sight of mud when the tide went out. He himself said "Get on with the dam across the Creek".

Battle now being joined, J.N.E. said that "He hesitated to suggest anything that might put a farthing on the rates, but improvements must come". An 'Ex-Ferrumite' chipped in to declare that the idea of a dam was farcical.

Things were getting heated. "Sir, this dam business seems to be developing somewhat, so far two against and three for, and if W.J.R. learned to swim without a dam, surely so could others," says P.G.

'Interested' now enters the lists. "Who is to awake Fareham and how? We need a dam and a hospital. Is Fareham so very poor or merely apathetic?"

A resident of a house overlooking the Creek spoke of her horror of perpetual high water with the din of speedboats all day — "Fareham Creek has a charm all of its own."

The last word seems to have been with P.G.: "Those who use the Creek most do not want this dam scheme at all. What is needed is some dredging, a place where boats can be reached at high and low tide, and the area around to have flower beds and seats." Was he foreseeing the later 1980s? Anyway, for a time, apathy and oblivion once more set in.

North Of The Town

Turning to the north of the town, we find a different type of industrial activity, one that had gone on for generations and was to be closely connected with the Port of Fareham. This was the brick, tile and pottery industry which, although important, was to fade out between the two world wars. The Second World War was to prove disastrous for the local brick industry.

All the same apart from extra houses, North Hill was to remain substantially the same until the 1970s. Part way down was a swampy area, the remains of an old clay pit, which was destined to remain until relatively recently. It, too, has now disappeared under houses.

Mention has already been made to the infilling of old clay pits and their use for buildings and Mr. Sandy's fine garden, but we must remember that there were a large number of smaller kilns and that some old cottages were built of bricks 'burnt' on the spot.

Fareham and its surroundings were for many years to dominate the local industries with the famous 'Fareham Reds'. As well as being used locally on

North Hill – just before the 1914 War and it did not change much until the 1970s.

69

the forts, the old Queen Alexandra Hospital, Haslar Hospital as well as bridges, viaducts, local houses and cottages, the bricks were exported abroad, to make the Town Hall in Cape Town for example. Millions of the Fareham bricks went to London, forming the interior bricks of most pre-war buildings and had been used to build the Royal Albert Hall and the old St. Thomas' Hospital.

Unfortunately, the seam of greensand to be found in the now Green Hollow Close ran out and a new form of firing had to be developed. There were kilns along Wickham Road, Old Turnpike, Kiln Road, Holly Grove, Crocker Hill, Furze Hill, North Hill, Fareham Common, Redlands Lane and near the railway station — and a little further away were those of Fontley and Wallington.

Some manufacturers, for example Mr. Sandy, concentrated also on fine pottery and terra-cotta, making reproductions also of antique pottery and assisting the British Museum.

A delightful story is told of a retired Colonel who sent to the pottery for an expert to copy a rare and ancient Egyptian vase. The colonel closely questioned the potter as to his qualifications whereupon the potter replied calmly that, when the work was finished, the two vases would be indistinguishable since he himself had actually made the 'Egyptian' vase he was being

Brick kiln at North Hill.

The Fareham potter who appeared on BBC TV after the Second World War. He worked for Mr. Sandy.

asked to copy. The Colonel was extremely annoyed having paid a large sum for the vase in Egypt, where he had been assured that it was genuine. He was not convinced until shown the private mark of the craftsman at the base of the vase. His language could not be recorded.

Up Old Turnpike was an old clay pipe industry linked with the Goodall family. Pipes and broken bits are still to be found in the gardens. Harris, of Fareham Common, was known for chimney pots, and North Hill brickworks were known for their specialised work, even though later they went back to clay pots and drainpipes.

The potteries also had the kudos of providing the potter in one of the 'Interludes' on BBC Television.

Between the wars, the industry in general declined and it must be said that sighs of relief went up from motorists driving along Kiln Road, as they had frequently had to drive blindly through smoke when the wind was in the wrong direction. The North Hill Potteries did continue on a smaller scale and two of the kilns remained. The size of the man shown in one of the photographs gives us an idea of the size of the kilns — there was far more below the surface than above. They were eight feet thick and it took one ton of coal to make two thousand bricks.

It is pleasant to know that these potteries continued after World War Two. Hand made bricks, flower pots and drain pipes were being made when the potteries were bought out and were transferred to Denmead. Back came the old skills, bricks were placed on an assembly line and the potters concentrated on high quality goods. They broke into the London market with a week's demonstration at Harrods and then entered the American market.

Now the area is built on but the potters' cottages are easily recognisable in Old Turnpike, Kiln Road and North Hill.

At the bottom of North Hill, Mitchener's Pond was always a healthy lake in a former clay pit standing near the entrance to Hellyers Farm. It had a permanent water supply and was well known as a skating spot in severe winters. (It was later to disappear with the arrival of the M27. Twice in severe weather it has re-asserted itself to flood the road and cut off Fareham's northern exit. This to the unholy joy of 'Ferrumites', who always did say that the M27 should have been placed further north!)

Between the wars there was a great deal of housing development and it is difficult to realise how 'open' was the land surrounding the old roads, which were often only lanes and around the kilns. Perhaps a look over the long hedge in Kiln Road gives the best idea. From here can still be seen the lands of Kneller Court, Roche Court whose lands stretch as far as North Fareham; Hellyers, Dean, Charity, Heytesbury, Albany and Knowle farms. Much of Fareham Common has now been built over, but it was very extensive and linked up with Wickham Commons.

Here is again a link up with Redlands Lane in Fareham because of the 'travellers' who were to be found all around the district. Between the wars, some of them were beginning to put down their roots. One of the best known travellers was Manny Golby, son of a family who had settled. Manny served in the Army during the Great War, was mentioned in despatches and was awarded the D.C.M. He saved his major's life and they both used to meet annually at Manny's house.

Manny's wife was Charlotte Birch, sister of Nelson Birch who lived in the Radlands Lane and Mill Road area of Fareham. Her grandmother, another Charlotte, was also the grandmother of Joe Beckett. She brought Joe into the world in a horse drawn caravan. He went on to become British heavyweight boxing champion, but it was said by those who knew them that Joe's brother, George, could give Joe a hiding when he liked, but did not take up boxing professionally because he liked his pint of beer too much!

During the 1920s and 1930s the seasonal 'travellers' used to arrive regularly in the area. Seven or eight horse drawn caravans used to come to Fontley every year and the caravans were pitched in the farmyard at Hope Farm at the bottom of Fontley Hill. They worked mainly on Dean Farm and Hope

Michener's Pond was destroyed when the M27 was built.

Farm. After the seasonal work was over they left for Alton for the hop picking. Over the years, more families stayed in and around the area buying an acre or two of ground, living in their caravan and doing many odd jobs. In the winter they cut cord wood and logs and made fencing posts and pegs. If there was no other work they would go around selling clothes pegs, bunches of wild flowers and watercress. True travellers or gypsies are rarely seen nowadays.

If we continue away from Fareham along Kiln Road, we come to another steep hill, this time Fontley Hill leading past the old Church and school into the hamlet of Fontley — or Funtley, if you wish to quibble! Mr. Percy Bennett, the school Headmaster, insisted upon the 'U'. The inhabitants, however, insist on Fontley, backing up their claim with Great and Little Fontley farms and Fontley tiles which are actually stamped with the name. If one wishes to be pedantic, both versions are correct!

The Dairy at Fontley – 'Rose Bank' and the Miners' Arms are in the back-ground. The dairy was demolished about 1930 and three pairs of cottages, 'Hope Cottages', now stand on the site.

The Miners' Arms (about 1922-23). Left to right: Fred Day (attendant of Knowle Hospital), George Oakes (landlord of the Miners' Arms), George Feast, 'Cracker' Ford (attendant at Knowle).

Life At Fontley

(I am indebted to Mr. Fred Hoare for much personal material, photographs and details of the Fontley Brick and Tile Works — A.J.)

Fred Hoare was born at Fontley in 1920. His father, George Hoare, had been in the Royal Engineers as a young man, then went to Knowle Hospital as an attendant, only to be called up in 1914 as he was still on the Reserve List and also a trained nurse. When the war finished, he returned to the hospital and his first job was to drive a horse and cart to Fareham every morning to take the mail in, pick up mail from the Post Office and take and pick up any parcels from the railway station. He also dealt with any other messages and shopping required. On Thursdays, he picked up the money from the bank for the staff wages when he always had another attendant to help him. The last winter that the horse and cart were used, there was a heavy fall of snow and a horse drawn snow plough from the hospital got him to and from Fareham.

About 1927, the hospital bought its first van, a chain-driven Morris and the horse and cart were dispensed with. Doctor Jackson, the hospital Superintendent, taught Mr. Hoare to drive and he retired from the hospital in 1940 after thirty-five years service.

In the 1920s, all village children started their schooling in the Reading Room at the foot of Fontley Hill and at the age of six they moved to the main school on the side of Fontley Hill near the Church.

In 1925, Fred started to go to the Sunday School at Fontley Reading Room which was in the charge of Mrs. Sutton, of Maylings House. By 1929, she was very infirm and ten of the boys used to go up to her house every Sunday afternoon. A kind, generous lady, she gave Christmas parties and games and parties in her gardens in summer — "But for her, we would not have had a party to go to in our young lives," Fred declared.

The extension to the main day school was finished in 1926 just when Fred moved up. His Headmaster was Mr. Percy Bennett. School sports were held at Maylings House.

From 1929 on, all children when eleven years of age had to go to Fareham for their last three years of schooling. Fred went to the Senior Boys' School in Gordon Road and later moved to the new school in Harrison Road in 1932.

Farming and life in general was labour intensive and children were expected to do their share of the work. At the age of eight, Fred set off with six cans every morning to walk across Fontley Common to Hellyers Farm where he collected the milk for six families in Fontley Lane. He left home at 7.30, collected and delivered the milk, got back for breakfast and then went off to school. Each family gave him threepence a week for this. As a boy he sang in Fontley Church Choir, earning two shillings and sixpence a year and having an annual outing. In 1930, he moved to Knowle Hospital Church and was very pleased as the choir boys were paid five shillings a year! In 1931, he progressed to the Senior Boys' School and was given his first bicycle.

Cecil Ray, who lived in Fontley Lane, left Fareham school as Fred started. Cecil had been doing the Evening News paper round from the top of North Hill along Kiln Road and through the village to the water works at the top of River Lane, so Fred took it over. He was paid three shillings and sixpence a week for it. Although Saturday was technically a holiday, it was, in fact, a busy day with many errands and chores to do. Sunday, of course, was church and choir; Monday, a heavy wash day; but for the Hoare children, Friday evenings meant that they were allowed to go to see the silent films at Knowle Hospital, where seats were set aside for children of the staff.

About 1930-31 an Air Show by Alan Cobham was held in the big field between Fontley and Knowle. This was known as the 'Back' field. The charge for a flight was five shillings.

Fontley people in 'Snobby' Goddall's charabanc on a trip to Southsea in 1919.

FONTLEY SCHOOL

Above: 1919-20; below, 1920-21.

Above: 1924-25; below, 1927-28.

Yet another Fontley School picture. When?

79

Fred spent a lot of his spare time at Dean Farm, with Reg Webb, helping with haymaking and harvesting. Here they had a report of the 1929 Schneider Trophy Race. All the traffic on the main roads was nose to tail and stationary right back to Droxford and to Waltham Chase, so they made their way to the large concrete water towers at Red Barn Farm and from there had a wonderful view of the race.

Fred left school in 1934 to work as a 'run about' boy with the firm building Ravenswood House. One of his jobs was to take the tools to be sharpened at the Forge at Wickham. The House being built, he found himself jobless — "if you lived in Fontley, if you didn't work at the Brick and Tile Works, you didn't work anywhere". But he found work there, stayed until the war when he was in the Army and ended up as being one of the last people to leave the Brick and Tile Works when it closed in 1946.

This, therefore, was the typical life of a boy growing up in Fontley between the wars. It was hard, but not without many amusements and activities.

The Social Club came into being in the early 1920s, the original building being a wartime structure obtained from Roche Court. Among many activities there were the 'Tanner Hops' — sixpenny dances on Saturday nights. In extremely cold weather there was ice skating and a good slide on the clay pit ponds. In summer there was swimming in the river Meon at Dead Man's Hole. Charabanc outings were frequent, and there were Sunday School treats and socials.

Below: Ice skating (1927-28) on the small brickyard pond at the rear of the school at Fontley Hill. In this mixture of village school children and Brick and Tile workers (who could not work because the clay was frozen) are Reginald 'Flash' Stocks (in foreground) with Fred Hoare (in overcoat) just behind.

Warmer days – 1932: Fontley and Knowle lads in the River Meon at Dead Man's Hole.

Outside the old Fontley Social Club in the 1930s. Left to right: back row; 'Ham' Bone, Mrs. Jukes, Natty Adams, Jimmy Farley, Bill Jukes. Front row; Percy 'Maddock' Adams, Fred Adams and Archie Kingswell.

In 1934, a visit to the Crystal Palace was arranged with both Fontley and Fareham people.

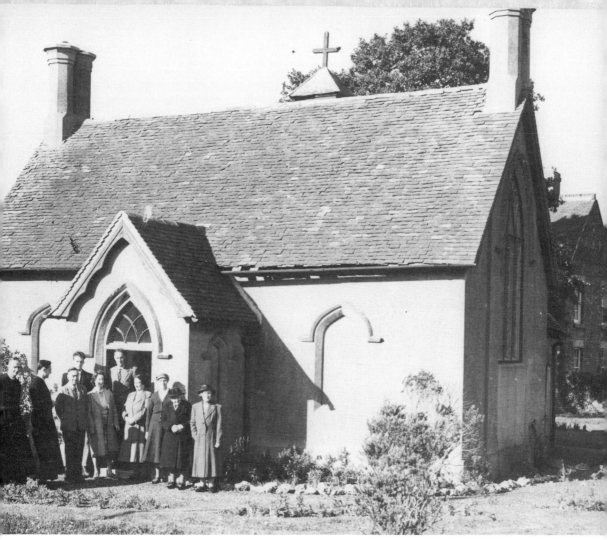

In 1936 the little church of St. Francis celebrated its centenary.

It is impossible to refer to Fontley without mentioning the Miners Arms. It was built by the great grandfather of Fred Hoare, a George Feast. There is also a link up here with Wallington, as Saunders the brewers came from there. The public house got its name at the time when the railway tunnel was being put through. The navvies, who were mainly Welsh miners, actually named the pub when one of them picked up a piece of chalk, went outside and wrote on the wall 'The Miners Arms'. The brewers agreed to the name.

Another link with Fareham came when Charlie Smith started the Fareham, Fontley to Knowle bus service in 1926. Incidentally he also was to become the inn keeper at the 'Miners'. There have only been five landlords in 150 years.

It must be remembered that in many ways life at Fontley was reflected in life in Fareham. The church was linked to the main Fareham parish church, the older children went to school in Fareham and there was the inevitable link up in farming with the Fareham Market, and in industry.

Many of us, whether living in the area or not, remember the delivery vans and what were to become the mobile shops. During the period between the wars we have a record of many of these people.

Harry Scorey lived in an old thatched cottage in Turnpike and stabled his horse between the New Inn and the Post Office. He delivered coal in his horse drawn cart. Jock White, who lived at the Quay (Fareham), sold wet fish from his horse and trolley; while Rupert Wheeler actually brought the bread round from Portchester. Milk was delivered from the dairy in the village by Mr. Hands and Dick Wetherhead also delivered milk for his father from Bridge Farm at the top of River Lane. He used to carry two milk cans on the handlebars of his bike and ladle it out into the customers' jugs.

Lusby's, of Fareham, also delivered. Miss Gill came for the grocery orders on Mondays and the groceries were delivered by van on Fridays. Mr. Warwick, of Wickham, and also a Mr. Hogg, delivered paraffin and meths. for the oil lamps and primus stoves. They also sold all kinds of hardware.

Ruben Nash came around selling meat. His shop was near the Post Office at the top of Turnpike. On Saturdays there were three regular tradesmen. Mr. Farrow sold all kinds of kindling wood. His farm was in Maylings Farm Road. Mr. Knocker visited the village carrying two large suitcases and selling clothes — two shillings down and one shilling a week after. Frankie Carter sold stale cakes from Pyle's bakery. He had two big baker's baskets slung over his shoulder.

There was the inevitable rag and bone man with his donkey and cart who stabled his donkey at the rear of the Royal Oak; Fareham. He got the nickname of Twister by being caught taking empty beer bottles from the back of the Royal Oak and in through the front door to get the deposit money again!

Mr. Jack Spanner was virtually Fontley's last lamplighter and could be seen at dusk lighting first the oil lamps and in later years the gas lamps. Through the day he was known in Fareham as a window cleaner. Biddy Kinch, from Titchfield, sold winkles, cockles and eels. There was the occasional arrival of an Italian with his barrel organ and once or twice a year, Mr. Ince, a well known figure in Fareham and Fontley, would come round with his three wheeled, highly polished machine to sharpen all the knives and scissors.

Right: 1928;
Charlie Smith's 14-seater bus.
Below: May, 1935;
Charlie Smith's three buses decorated with flags for the silver Jubilee of King George V and Queen Mary with the buses are George Gates (landlord, Miners' Arms), Mrs. Cook, of Yew Tree Cottages, and Charles Adams (Brickyard clay pit worker).

Fontley Brick and Tile Works – 1923
Tiles being loaded onto a railway wagon from a tile bogie at Fontley Works Railway siding.
Left to right: Jack Watts, Tom Fleet and Ern Morris. Extreme right; Percy Adams from
Union Street, Fareham.

Fontley Brick and Tile Works – Grading Tiles 1923/24
Left to right: R. Perrior, H. Carlton, P. Carter, A. Wild, R. Hulbert.

Fontley Brick and Tile Works

Just as Fontley **was** originally the Iron Works, so it later became **the** Brick and Tile Works for the district. At a rough count the photograph of the work force shows at least 130, not forgetting the dog!

The Fontley Hand Brick Making Yard was opposite the present Fontley abbatoir and stood in Fontley Copse. Hand made bricks from here went to build Ravenswood House at Knowle Hospital and, in Fareham itself, the Hants and Dorset bus station, the front of the Embassy Cinema; Burpham House, Bath Lane; Lynton House, High Street; the Victory public house, and the Magistrates' Court in Trinity Street, and the West End public house.

The clay here is London Blue and shrinks when dried so loam from the top of the copse had to be mixed with it to keep the bricks the correct size. It was then put through the Pug-mill with the required amount of water and the Pug-boy had to break off lumps of clay from the column of pug and throw it into a skip for the brickmakers. Before the invention of the pug-mill, handbrick and tile makers had to 'tread their own clay' with their bare feet. After this they made 1,100 bricks daily, the odd hundred to make up for any time lost through wet weather during the week. It must have been an exhausting 12 hour day.

The bricks were then put on 'Acks' which were strips of board about 50 yards in length, covered by wooden 'Cops' to keep the rain off and with strips of wood standing at the side. The Acks were long enough to take a day's work. Next day the bricks were dry enough to take the weight of the next day's work. The limit was six high and after drying out for ten days they were 'skintled', that is the bricks were turned outside in to dry evenly.

There were two 'Scotch Kilns' in which the bricks were set to be burnt and in all there were about 25 rows high. The bricks were burnt a different colour according to their position in the kiln.

After the invention of the pug-mill a Ruston Hornsby engine was used to drive it. Its nickname was the 'Donkey' (The old fly-wheel has been found recently and will be set up at Fareham Museum). During the winter months the brickmakers were incorporated into the Main Yard in the village where they worked on the tiles and machine made bricks.

Machine made bricks were not made at Fontley until about 1923. During the Great War, cordite was stored in the kilns and drying sheds and the workers were Fontley women. They wore rough clothes (and actually trousers!) and heavy boots.

When the wire cut brick making machine was installed, a large drying shed was built and it stretched from opposite 1, Hope Cottages to Cressy Cottages. The huge 'continuous kiln' was also built and reached from the end of the drying shed to nearly opposite the Miners Arms. It held almost one million bricks when full and until the war years the kiln was never out. The bricks which were called 'Wire-Cuts' were produced ten at a time from the column of clay issuing from the pug-mill. The clay was exactly the right size of the bricks. They sold for thirty shillings a thousand.

Machine made tiles were being produced in the Brick and Tile Works before the 1914-18 war. There were ten round shaped kilns, each at different stages so that the flow of tiles was kept moving. The clay was from a dark red seam and it was almost rock hard. The face the men were working on was up to 20 feet high and the men would cut into the side of the face and underneath and before going home would drive in pieces of wood about three feet back from the top and tip in buckets of water. Hopefully by morning the clay would have slipped and broken itself up, but men were liable to take chances when doing this and over the years three men were killed by falls of clay.

The tiles were graded and carefully stacked. From the 1920s many thousands of tiles were loaded first from a tile bogey and then onto railway trucks, packed in straw and sent all over the country from Fontley railway siding.

Many also went by sea from Fareham Quay. During the 1920s and 1930s, wire-cuts from Belgium were brought into Fareham by barge and could be sold more cheaply than those made here. But Fontley workers did not mind as a barge load of tiles was always taken back to Belgium. On three occasions in the late 1930s Mr. Hoare was at the creek helping to load. It took a whole week to load a barge, with lorries continually running from Fontley from 7 a.m. until 5.30 p.m. or until noon on Saturday.

Looking from the road now, no-one would think that a thriving brick making industry stood there for many years.

These were the men who made the bricks and tiles.

Wallington

Always referred to in Kelly's Directory as 'a hamlet adjoining Fareham on the north east, with a brewery,' Wallington was and is much more than that. During the period between the wars there was a big fall in industries, for Wallington had had a big tannery (Sharland's), an important pottery industry (Stares), and a large brewery. Fortunately, the latter under Messrs H. H. and R. J. Saunders still thrived.

The panoramic post card shows Wallington as it was to remain between the wars with Broadcut leading away before the bridge, the Tavern and the ford by the bridge which was kept open for horses and carts to be driven in to be washed.

In times of high tide and especially when combined with heavy rain it was common for flooding to occur around Broadcut, along Wallington Shore Road and for the water to pour through the cottages. This can still happen. A one time resident, selling his more modern house in the 1960s, was asked whether the river ever flooded. "I can't say it does," came the reply, only for small daughter to butt in with "But Daddy, remember when the dustbin floated out of the front gate?".

The river Wallington is actually tidal to Wallington bridge.

The cottages by the bridge at North Wallington have remained almost unchanged

Drift Road. Although today the road has been improved, the scene has changed little in the past 60 years.

The great Mill Pond did not silt up until after the 1930s; Wallington had quays along it and there was a tunnel under the A27 bridge for barges to go through. The Fareham Sailing Club proved that this navigation was still possible in 1938 when several dinghies made their way through to Wallington bridge and back to Fareham.

There were several large houses in Wallington — Wallington House occupied by the Coppinger family, The Tanneries by the Sharlands, Mrs. King was at Wallington Hill House, East Hill was occupied by Rev. W. Hamilton, and Captain Larking, R. N., was at Wallington Lodge. There was also St. Edith's House, a Church of England home for girls between the ages of 14 and 16 years. They were trained for potential service in the larger houses and learnt housework, laundry and cooking. Later there were younger children who went to the Church of England School in Osborn Road (St. Edith's is now disguised as the Roundabout Hotel).

After the Sharland family left the tannery, the land was to change hands several times and there was always a small amount of tanning going on. The tannning sheds came down in the 1930s, when there was a gale. Fires were dealt with from Fareham, thankfully in those days there was no one-way road system for communications could be a problem.

Wallington House.

St. Edith's Home and Mill Pond (1929).

Roasting the Ox at the fair once organised by Wallington in the Old Manor Meadow.

The brewery was still going strong and there were — and still are — two public houses, the White Horse and the Fort Wallington Tavern, a reminder that Fort Wallington on top of the hill was still in Army occupation. The modern change of name of the latter to the Cob and Pen destroyed this historical link. No doubt the public houses were patronised by the soldiers whose laundry was done by Wallington women.

During this period, therefore, Wallington seemed a rather quiet back water and a wonderful place to wander around with its river, water meadows and farms. It led its own quiet life with its annual fair, fete, flower show, carnival and water gala. For the latter, held opposite the White Horse, the river which was usually about three feet deep was dammed in two places so that competitions could be held. Most popular among the spectators at least were probably the greasy poles and there were many muddy duckings. The carnival was enjoyed by the people of Wallington and Fareham but it has to be said that the Fareham visitors were never particularly welcome! Wallington had and still has a strong community spirit and like so many small communities in Hampshire, liked to keep to itself.

Opposite Top: These Wallington cottages were pulled down to make way for the M27.
Middle: Behind the Wallington brewery. Bottom: Wallington River with Broadcut alongside.

A VIEW AT WALLINGTON

24 WALLINGTON RIVER, NORTH-FAREHAM

The 1937 Coronation celebration – all the children of Wallington were told 'everyone bring a cup and plate'.

Schools

Fareham, like many other towns in the past fifty years, has been celebrating school centenaries. Sometimes the children have commemorated the event by dressing in period dress and to see them playing up Old Turnpike road during the lunch hour was rather like seeing a 'Stuart' post card come to life.

We have many log books, minutes and Managers' reports to draw on during this period, so it is only possible to give samples of life in the schools.

What does come through is the heartbreaking amount of poverty, ill health and frequency of dangerous diseases which simply had to run their course. In spite of these difficulties, the standard achieved in basic subjects was often higher than it would be today. For instance, the infants were expected to know their 'three R's', do simple sewing and also learn to knit. All this before seven years of age. Quite a task for the teachers, considering the problem of the numerous absences.

Oldest of all the schools was the once Charity School of Price's. Brought into being in 1721 by the will of William Price, it was to have a distinguished record throughout its 250 years.

Well before the end of the Great War, Price's was settled in Park Lane. Such was the feeling about the school that, as Mr. R. Daysh, both a pupil and a member of staff, was to say "One tends to think that there have been thousands of boys who went to Price's School up to 1939, but in fact, there were only 1,337. There were many Priceans who achieved eminence in one sphere or another and there is no doubt at all that the School owed its fine reputation to its staff. In those days masters took a post meaning to stay there. Both Mr. Bradley, the first headmaster at Park Lane, and Mr. Ashton who succeeded him in 1934, selected men as much for their personal qualities as well as for their academic ones.

"For this period, we might mention three well known pupils. R. A. Lewry (1921-28) was a great footballer going straight into the first XI as a second-former. His reputation became so formidable that visiting opponents would enquire anxiously 'is Lewry still here?'. Another great footballer was W. J. Tubbs (1933-39), daunting in stature. We must not fail to mention J. C. Draper (1929-33) who became known to thousands of Hampshire people as an authority on local history, Hampshire flora and Hampshire and British geology."

In 1921, Price's celebrated its bi-centenary and in 1923 the school War Memorial was dedicated by the headmaster of Winchester College.

Price's hockey team of 1921.

Games were always a part of the curriculum. A high standard was achieved, all the staff being expected to take a share in organising games. In the 1930s the school pitch was considerably improved by Mr. Johnston setting boys to work digging out plantains at a rate of sixpence per hundred. Price's Sports Day will be remembered by many for Mr. Shaw starting the races by firing blanks from his .303 Cadet rifle — they never did have a proper starting pistol!

The arrival of the Senior Girls' School in Harrison Road was to give Mr. Bradley some qualms. He felt that the boundary fence must be repaired — "so that it could effectively be closed at night". What did he think the boarders would get up to?

The school magazine, always known as the *Lion*, can produce some amusing and useful quotes:

1925. 'A ride on a Gosport tram is not meant for comfort or for those in a hurry — if they are in a hurry, they walk.'

1926. 'The *Lion* was one of the few periodicals whose publication was not interfered with by the General Strike!'

1928. 'The arrival of the new style PT created much alarm for it was considered

98

Price's teaching staff in the 1930s.

R. E. Garton, B. R. Shaw, F. H. Brown, Miss V. M. Jewel, M. R. Thacker, J. Lockhart, T. W. Foster, J. Shaddock, R. O. Johnston, Miss E. A. D. Bourchier, S. R. N. Bradly, (Headmaster 1908-34), Mrs. S. R. N. Bradly, A. S. Gale, P. W. Mundy.

that boys in the fifth form would require all their time to study so it was really quite a delight to reach the upper forms, in order to watch other less brainy individuals exerting themselves and suffering considerable physical strain.'

When Mr. Shaddock finally retired, the magazine commented 'he has always been seen as enduring as a piece of the landscape'.

Price's was an 'all round' school, fitting its boys for all walks of life and sending increasing numbers to the universities. It was a sad day when it became a co-educational Sixth Form College, even sadder when the name 'Price's' was dropped from the notice board and saddest of all when it was moved lock, stock and barrel to the Bishopsfield campus site. What has happened to the sense of history?

Although Price's Charity laid down that there should be an equal number of girls and boys in the school, by 1820 the girls had 'disappeared', and they were to wait for a Grammar School until the latter part of the 1950s.

Mr. G. Ashton,
the Headmaster.

Price's School in 1937.

The School's Cadet Force
on the playing fields.

Below: Main Buildings.

100

FAREHAM SCHOOLS

Gordon Road Boys' School – 1925

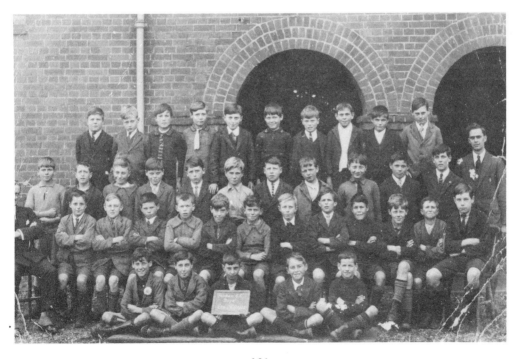

Church of England Girls' School – 1926.

Gordon Road Boys' School with Mr. Mortimer (Headmaster) – 1927.

Two Junior Forms of Wickham Road School, 1930.

Gordon Road School performed 'HMS Pinafore' in 1927.
Below: Fareham Secondary Boys' School, 1932.

Fareham County Primary School, on the Wickham Road, celebrated its centenary by the publication of a delightful booklet called 'In the Beginning', compiled by Mr. Betenson and Mrs. Stokes. It was, in fact, to record the beginning of two schools. There were on the site the Infants and the Girls School. Across the passageway was the Church of England School.

With the availability of records by the headmistresses and managers one gets a clear picture of conditions of work, health and absenteeism. Stormy weather lowered attendances as did flooding at Wallington. All too frequently the schools were closed because of infectious diseases which included the dreaded scarlet fever and diphtheria. There were also moans from the staff about absenteeism due to the Fair, Fetes, Circuses and fruit picking and "why cannot all the Sunday School treats be held on the same afternoon?".

The Attendance Officer was zealous in his duties although perhaps the boys' school had more need of him than did the girls'!

The records show a holiday on Armistice Day and a week's full attendance by a form gained them a half day's holiday. The year 1923 was dreadful for ill health and the Inspector comments "work very creditable considering all the problems". In 1926, shoes were given by the Fareham Brotherhood for those who had none and this was to happen on several occasions. In 1929 there was a lecture on Alcohol and Muscular Power by the Band of Hope! The senior girls were only fourteen and were due to leave school. Obviously it was thought wise to warn them of the perils of the 'demon drink'.

In 1930, the school closed to re-open as a Junior Mixed Department while the Seniors went on to the new school in Harrison Road. This school was to gather children from a wide catchment area. Miss Ings, who had been headmistress, went on to Harrison Road and was destined to teach in the two schools for forty-five years. She started with 240 on the books and in 1932 remarked on the building of the new boys' school. The next year was to see the start of hot dinners twice weekly for those who had long distances to travel and hot milky drinks were supplied daily.

The wireless was becoming a part of school life. Broadcast lessons were reported in 1934 when Sir Walford Davies welcomed the school as new listeners to the music lessons!

Parents were beginning to agree to the girls staying on beyond their fourteenth birthday and 1935 showed over 400 on the Roll and insufficient seating provided. The year was also to give school holidays for two Royal Weddings and the King's Silver Jubilee. It was also to provide one of the worst storms in living memory, when high gales, thunder and torrential rain brought down trees which blocked the roads and prevented children from reaching school. There was less excuse in 1936 when the headmistress stated "numbers decreased in spite of the beautiful weather. Very few have a legitimate excuse for absence".

Above: Fareham Church of England Junior School, 1938. Standard 4.
Back row: Rosemary Stead, Madeline Thornton, Jack Hill, Betty Moore, Audrey Hewett,
Norman Lawrence, Sheila Feast, Sheila Bull. Second row from back: Nancy Brace, Patrick
Keefe, Hazel Morris, Arthur Wassell, Joyce Hayward, Don Wells, Mary Wassell, John
Jupe, Iris Francis, Maurice Lemm. Third row from back: Iris Cottle, Chris Wright, Irene
Hockey, Alan Hewlett, Hazel Warnekey, Kenneth Marchant, Barbara Godfray, Roy Lacey,
Irene Lewis, Raymond Freeman, Barbara Watts. Second row from front: Eileen Cooper,
Richard Adams, Barbara Pearce, Albert Coffin, Joyce Searle, Alec Bowmaker, Marjorie
Underwood, Sidney Marsh, Roma Coombes, Neville Olden, Christine Player, Michael Moss,
Sheila Jarman (standing). Front row: Beatrice Barnard, Maureen Wareham, Joyce Woodnutt,
Kathleen Wassell, Betty Barker, Alan March, Jim Holbrook, ? Street, Gordon Rees.

Staff of Fareham Senior Girls' School, Harrison Road, 1939.
Back row: Miss Collins, Mrs. Rothwell, Miss Williams, Miss Fisher, Miss Avery
(Cookery), Mrs. Wilson. Front row: Mrs. Raynor, Mrs. Renshaw, Miss Belben, Miss Ings
(Headmistress), Miss Gentry, Miss Swinbank, Miss Nuttall.

War clouds were gathering and there was tension here as in all the other schools.

The school meals service was to become a regular feature but some chaos was occurring at the beginning, "as the equipment ordered three months ago has not arrived, it is impossible to organise the dinners. Today the girls were each carrying a plate of stew, across the playground in torrential rain".

Then came 1939, the summer holidays and World War Two.

Opposite page: lower picture.
Left to right; back row: Chris Wright, Beatie Bachelor, Betty Moore, Donald Wells, Mary Wassell, Betty Barker, Neville Olden. Second row from back: Gwen Aylott, Trixie Moth, Brenda Gates, Ralph Oliver, Barbara Coates, Albert Coffin. Third row from back: Jean Samways, Jean Carter, Joyce Bond, Roy Lacey, John Jupe, Kathleen Wassell, Alan Hewlett, Nancy Brace, Barbara Watts. Second row from front: Madelaine Thornton, Jack Hill, Beatrice Barnard, Iris Francis, Michael Moss, Joyce Searle, Walter Gee, Patrick Keefe, Iris Cottle. Front row: Sidney Marsh, Joyce Hayward, Maureen Wareham, Marjorie Underwood, ? Lloyd, Joan Warner, Jim Massey.
(These names were first published in the News, Portsmouth on July 28, 1989).

Doubtless similar minutes were recorded for the Senior Boys' School although perhaps there were more records of canings! All boys went to this school at the age of eleven. When it opened it was in School Road but the name of the road was to be altered to Gordon Road and the school had been known as the Gordon Road Academy. It was a fine building with 'arches around the ground floor to shelter under if it was raining'.

Once again we know that the masters were strict but fair, that they stayed and gave continuity and that the amount of work done was sound and gave the boys an excellent start in life. They suffered the same problems of absenteeism through ill health and various activities of Fareham life and there was more truancy, especially on Mondays.

One time pupils speak with appreciation of the work done, of the staff (some of whom are still around) and of plays and concerts being given.

Once again there is the realisation of the problems of distances to be travelled, often on foot or bike.

In 1931, as the winter started, the Y.M.C.A. began selling soup at dinner time for the children. A small basin of soup called 'skilly' cost 1d and bread was ½d a slice (old currency). One old boy comments "If the weather was bad, I had two pennies for soup and two slices of bread. It was much better than cycling home and getting wet through'.

In 1932, the school was to move to the new Fareham Senior Boys' School in Harrison Road. The pattern of education was to be the same as at the Girls' School with the introduction of the wireless and broadcast lessons and the start of school meals. The same old pupil comments "a hot drink was provided at morning break, it was Horlicks and it cost 1d a cup".

The outbreak of war in 1939 was to interrupt the lives of these boys. Indeed many of those who had been at school in 1933 were immediately called up to join one of the Foreces.

Private Schools

At this period there were also private schools in the district. Two in particular stand out, St. Fillans and Wykeham House.

St. Fillans was started at 6, Southampton Road by Mrs. Porter and was for young boys as well as for girls. Mrs. J. Harper was a pupil there for five or six years until it closed in 1935. "The Headmistress was Miss Jesse Porter and she was assisted by her sister Miss Norah, while Miss Edith acted as housekeeper and cared for their aged mother. There was another sister, Deaconess Blanche Porter, who was a missionary in Madagascar for many years.

Peter and Paul Church: are you on it?

"The school uniform was navy blue with S.F.F. in bright yellow on our blazer badges and smaller ones on our black velour hats. The school was mainly for junior pupils although a few girls remained into their secondary schooling years. I suppose there were thirty pupils, and several different age groups were taught by Miss Porter in one large room, while Miss Norah took the youngest children separately . . . No doubt the teaching was given on old-fashioned and traditional lines with emphasis on the 'three R's' and giving a good groundwork in the basic subjects. I remember my introduction to Shakespeare was listening to the seniors reading 'Julius Caesar' and 'Romeo and Juliet' while *our* group was writing in our copy-books in copperplate writing. I still recall the first page of that book stating 'Ait, an island in a river' which has since proved a useful piece of information for crossword puzzles! There was a visiting elocutionist and a Miss Tonkins visited the school to teach games and P.E. For this we were taken to a field belonging to the Misses Sharland in Osborn Road on the site of the present multi-storey car park."

Wykeham House School still thrives. Over the years it had changed its name according to the premises occupied. It started at Orme Lodge under Mrs. Baylis and in 1918 moved further along West Street to Western House where Mrs. Baylis remained in charge until 1923. As she wished to retire, the school was advertised for sale and was looked over by Miss Alsop. She said "Mrs. Baylis took me into the garden where there was a big tennis court of which most of Fareham seemed to be proud. I thought it was a very nice school and that I should like it for my own, so I went back to London to think about it and after a time, came back with Miss Falvell to look again and we took over the school in May 1923".

The school was to move again to Wykeham House, 69 High Street, in 1928. After the death of Miss Flavell, Miss Alsop continued until her retirement in 1937. It was after Miss Alsop's retirement that there were two disastrous years when the school numbers dropped to 37.

In 1939 it was taken over by Mrs. Duff and Miss Beer and numbers rose to over 200.

Again it was to be a school with continuity of staff, a well balanced timetable and where the children made great progress. There was a small preparatory department for boys but girls stayed on often to take the then School Certificate examinations. Always commented upon was the warm and friendly atmosphere of the school, relaxed but well disciplined and several generations of the same families have passed through its hands. It did have a boarding section.

Competent and thoughtful teaching with members of staff expecting courtesy and consideration from the girls in their behaviour towards others made it a delightful school to know.

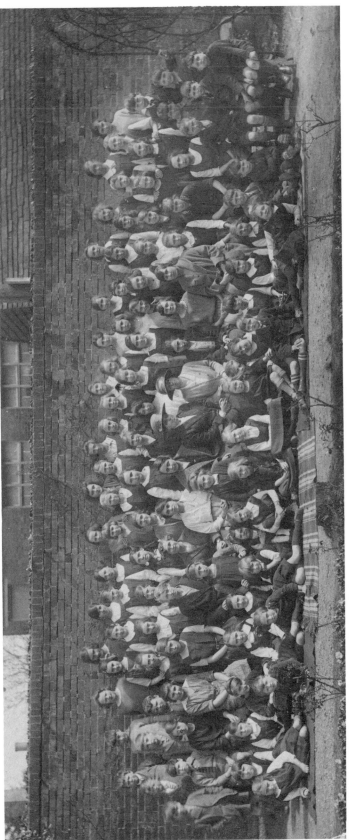

Western House School, 1929.

Fareham Cricket XI, 1935.
D. Bennett, L. Doodall, E. Norman, T. Wagstaffe, F. Troke, F. Bussey, H. Sturgess, S.
Wyatt, P. J. Bennett, A. Jones, A. Brewerton.
(Note from author: Sorry! I have neglected sport. Here are two pictures I have tucked in)

Fontley Football Club, 1937-38.

Conclusion

During the 1930s, we have seen that the whole tempo of life speeded up. So many changes had taken place in the world outside that no small town or village could remain unaffected.

A young generation had grown up which had taken no part in the Great War (1914-18) although it may have been affected by it in the loss of parents and relatives. Those who had returned safely were naturally determined to celebrate their safe deliverance, much seen in the larger towns with exotic stories of night clubs, Chelsea Balls and Boat Race nights.

In such towns as Fareham, people still made their own amusements, took part in plays and pageants, school trips and Sunday School outings, and with easier transport people ventured much further afield.

The motor car was here to stay and the roads in town were getting busy and even had parking problems! Cheap day returns by train and frequent services meant easy visits to London or to the seaside elsewhere. Buses ran regularly and often so that Portsmouth, Southampton and Winchester were in easy reach for the theatre, concerts and larger dances. There were many coaches to be hired for tours around the countryside.

Social life, at its different levels, had been resumed with regular invitations to tea parties, luncheon or dinner. There was no shortage of servants.

Radio might still be in its relative infancy and many wireless sets were home made, but portable wind-up gramophones were a part of life and mains electrically run radios and radiograms brought the most recent popular dance orchestra with the top tune of the moment into every home. Father insisted on the news bulletins! No longer was there any need to wait for the papers to find out about the Test Match, the Boat Race, Wimbledon or football internationals; one *listened* to the commentaries and if up sufficiently early, received the complicated commentaries on the Test Match in Australia.

The cinema was also all important. The two cinemas in Fareham often put on two feature films each every week *and* there were Junior Clubs on Saturdays. Teenagers collected film stars, not pop stars!

It was, of course, the radio and the cinema which was to warn us of the gathering storm clouds of war. In Fareham in 1937, the Territorial Army was drilling in their hall in Hartlands Road and the call went out for men and women volunteers for Civil Defence. Booklets were prepared and distributed — "what to do in case of air raids . . . gas attack, how to deal with 'black out', how to build up a store cupboard of food".

113

It was all going to begin again and although there were signs of relief at the breathing space given to us in 1938, gas masks were issued, shelters were built and buildings were protected by sandbags. The wireless broadcast the fateful news on September 3rd, 1939, news followed immediately by the air raid warning.

The older teenagers (of which the author was one) realised that *they* were going to be in the middle of a war; the lights were blacked out and once more life was never going to be the same again.

Few realized that six years would pass before the terrible conflict would end . . . before there would be happy V.E. Street Parties such as the one in Western Road below:

Acknowledgements

To all those readers, whose favourite memories of life in Fareham between the wars I have left out, my apologies. I must plead lack of space and hope that I may repair some of the omissions another time. Your memories are always welcome.

I must thank the many past and present residents of Fareham who have helped me — often unwittingly — to write this book. To be remembered with thanks are those old, past residents who first encouraged me in my local research. I shall always be grateful to Mr. George Privett, Mr. H. Privett, Mr. J. P. Garrad and Mr. J. C. Draper.

In strictly alphabetical order I must also thank the following for sending in their memories, giving information of past events and lending precious photographs:

Mrs. Baker	Mrs. Harper	Mr. M. Privett
Mr. & Mrs. Barfoot	Mrs. Hartley	Mr. Sawyer
Dr. Baulk	Mrs. Heaseman	Mrs. Sheaf
Mr. Betenson	Mr. Hoare	Mrs. Smith
Mrs. Billett	Mrs. Jones	Mr. S. S. Smith
Mrs. Bishop	Mrs. Knipe	Mrs. Stokes
Mrs. Briscoe	Mrs. Lawrence	Mr. Sturgess
Mrs. Budd	Mrs. Lewis	Mr. Swatton
Mrs. Clark	Mrs. Maye	Mr. Swinburne
Miss Crawshaw	Mrs. Mouland	Miss Thompson
Mr. Daysh	Mrs. Newton	Mrs. Varilone
Mrs. Etherington	Mr. Penfold	Mr. Vimpany
Mrs. Godwin	Mr. Perry	Mrs. Woolfrey
Mr. Grove	Mr. H. Privett	Mrs. Wright

Last but not least, my thanks to my husband, without whose typing and proof reading, this book could never have been produced.

Just one other point — a small number of the photographs were taken just before the 1914-18 war; but I selected them as they illustrated ideally the particular area which, in fact, was generally not altered until the 1960s.

A.J.

The Author

Mrs. Alice James (neé Hilton) was born in Lancashire and was educated in North Wales. At the beginning of the last war she went up to Newnham College, Cambridge, where she took an Honours Degree and collected a hockey Blue. She later played for the Southern Universities against Wales.

She came to Fareham at the beginning of the war, when it was a delightfully typical Hampshire market town. Her interest in local history had already been kindled at Cambridge, where the Geography Department had developed their course in Historical Geography.

Mrs. James, now retired, taught in Grammar and Public Schools in England and Canada; her last two posts being at Fareham Girls' Grammar School and finally as Headmistress of Wykeham House School.

With the partnership of colleagues, exhibitions of Local History were put on and aroused much interest and so she started the Fareham Local History Group which this year celebrates its 30th anniversary.

Through the years, aided and abetted by older Fareham residents, she has collected much material which otherwise might have been lost, and has built up a knowledge of the district. Realising the increasing demand for research material, the History Group started to produce booklets on research in 1965. These 'Fareham Past and Present' booklets have been brought out regularly bi-annually ever since.